SpringerBriefs in Psychology

School Psychology

More information about this series at http://www.springer.com/series/10143

Sara El Khoury • Anies Al-Hroub

Gifted Education in Lebanese Schools

Integrating Theory, Research, and Practice

Springer

Sara El Khoury
Department of Education
American University of Beirut
Jounieh, Lebanon

Anies Al-Hroub
Department of Education, Chairperson
American University of Beirut
Beirut, Lebanon

ISSN 2192-8363 ISSN 2192-8371 (electronic)
SpringerBriefs in Psychology
ISSN 2520-8918 ISSN 2520-8926 (electronic)
School Psychology
ISBN 978-3-319-78591-2 ISBN 978-3-319-78592-9 (eBook)
https://doi.org/10.1007/978-3-319-78592-9

Library of Congress Control Number: 2018937095

© The Author(s), under exclusive licence to Springer International Publishing AG, part of Springer Nature 2018
This work is subject to copyright. All rights are reserved by the Publisher, whether the whole or part of the material is concerned, specifically the rights of translation, reprinting, reuse of illustrations, recitation, broadcasting, reproduction on microfilms or in any other physical way, and transmission or information storage and retrieval, electronic adaptation, computer software, or by similar or dissimilar methodology now known or hereafter developed.
The use of general descriptive names, registered names, trademarks, service marks, etc. in this publication does not imply, even in the absence of a specific statement, that such names are exempt from the relevant protective laws and regulations and therefore free for general use.
The publisher, the authors and the editors are safe to assume that the advice and information in this book are believed to be true and accurate at the date of publication. Neither the publisher nor the authors or the editors give a warranty, express or implied, with respect to the material contained herein or for any errors or omissions that may have been made. The publisher remains neutral with regard to jurisdictional claims in published maps and institutional affiliations.

Printed on acid-free paper

This Springer imprint is published by the registered company Springer International Publishing AG part of Springer Nature.
The registered company address is: Gewerbestrasse 11, 6330 Cham, Switzerland

For my wonderful husband Vasilis; my amazing family Ishac, Ghada, and Jouana; and my cherished students
Sara El Khoury

To a very unique person in my life, to my father, Mohammad Al-Hroub
Anies Al-Hroub

Preface

In the fall of 2009, Anies Al-Hroub (the second author) conducted a research project on the utility of psychometric testing on identifying gifted children with learning disabilities in Lebanese schools. Part of the project included administering the Wechsler Intelligence Scale for Children (WISC) to students who were nominated by their school as being intellectually gifted. During the data collection, one student's mother contacted Al-Hroub inquiring as to how her son obtained a full-scale IQ of 116 on the WISC, when he scored 146 in the USA. This was a mystery, as this 12-year-old boy, whom we will refer to as Jad, was recognized as superiorly gifted in the United States, and while in Lebanon, his evaluation showed that he is intellectually average. The mother explained that Jad performed poorly on the IQ test on purpose. He feels more comfortable to hide his unbelievable knowledge and advanced academic abilities to "fit in" to the school. How could this be? Is there another choice for Jad?

Upon the mother's request, Al-Hroub conducted a number of interviews with Jad's teachers and mother. He also observed the child's academic performance at school, and reviewed documentary evidence, school reports, and home videos about Jad, in addition to psychoeducational evaluation reports provided by senior specialists in the Gifted Children Association of California (GCAC), USA. For further investigation, and while Sara El Khoury (the first author) and her colleagues were working toward their special education degree, at the American University of Beirut, Al-Hroub assigned them a task to further explore the case of Jad and uncover any possible areas of strengths and weaknesses. In order to assess the situation, the team conducted interviews with Jad's parents, and reviewed the documentary evidence including school performance and psychoeducational evaluation reports.

After a thorough review of the documentary evidence and home videos, Anies Al-Hroub and his team[1] arrived to the following:

At the age of two, Jad displayed an astonishing, immediate ability to identify all of the English alphabets, the English numbers from zero to twenty, colors, and different shapes (line, circle, square, rectangle, triangle, diamond, cube, cylinder,

---

[1] We thank Zainab El Bast and Lina Badra for their contribution.

exit and stop signs). Not only could he verbally identify the numbers and alphabets, but he could also write them. Concerning numbers and counting, Jad could count in Arabic, English, and French. At the age of three, Jad could correctly write a range of words including his name and names of animals and several objects (dogs, pigs, owls, house, circle, X-ray, umbrella, etc.). He could also write the English alphabets in the correct order. Jad successfully answered questions about word opposites. His parents would ask him about the opposites of certain words and he would answer very quickly; while writing the words down without spelling mistakes. In addition, he correctly wrote sentences such as "I love Dad." At the age of four, Jad could read English fluently without any difficulty. He was shown to be reading a science book explaining phenomena like lightning, rain, clouds, rainbows, and dew. He followed his father's orders to read louder and slower. He also demonstrated an extraordinary knowledge of the solar system, naming all the planets and pointing out their special characteristics (for example, Mars is the red planet, Uranus is too far). At the age of six – Grade 2, Jad rapidly progressed from Pre-K to second grade. For instance, when he was in KG2 (aged 4), he was able to learn the Arabic alphabets in just one day; a target that normally takes a year or more to be achieved. In grade 2, where he was the youngest in his class, he had excellent grades and completed his work with little or no effort. He was conversationally and academically fluent in English and his first language, Arabic. In grade 2, Jad was officially assessed and obtained a full IQ score of 146, which sets him at the 99th percentile, within the "very superior range" of intelligence for his chronological age. He demonstrated specific strengths in the domains of rote memory, arithmetic, reading, spelling, and spatial-visual relationships. In the testing situations, Jad seemed comfortable and self-confident. He maintained high levels of attention, concentration, and curiosity, responded insightfully and thoughtfully, and was appropriately persistent in completing tasks. Despite this, such results did not fully reflect his abilities as he consistently made connections between test items and his own experiences. Jad was identified as an exceptional student eligible for gifted and talented education programs.

At the age of 7–8, Grade 3, Jad took the California Standards Tests in English-Language Arts and Mathematics. He scored 368 in English Language Arts which is at the Proficient level and 452 in Mathematics which is at the Advance level. While in grade 3, Jad's math scores were comparable to those of an average seventh grader after the ninth month of the school year. Jad also achieved a national Percentile Rank (PR) of 99 which is higher than 99% of students nationally in the same grade. It was in this math test that Jad not only outperformed other gifted students, but also broke the record of the district of California for the past 65 years. Such scores meant that he understood most of the information in the K-8 basic math curriculum. In the same year, it was announced again that Jad meets State and District criteria for inclusion in the Gifted and Talented Education program in his school district. He had previously met the state-approved guidelines in his previous school district as well.

At the age of 9–10 – Grade 4, Jad received the President's Award for Educational Excellence with a letter of congratulation from The White House. Jad then took the California Standards Tests again in spring 2006 and his scores increased to 432 in

English-Language Arts, which is at the Advanced level and 520 in Mathematics, which is at the Advanced level as well. Such math scores showed that Jad's math skills are equal to those of post-high school students. During the 2005–2006 school year, Jad was placed in an advanced class with many other gifted students. He continued to do exceptional advanced work in math, English-Language Arts, social studies, and sciences (ranging from physical to life sciences). He had also grown in terms of his ability to relate to his peers. Instead of interrupting others, he started to value their input and respect the right of teachers to teach lessons thoroughly before asking questions or commenting. He was also learning to have empathy for others who are not as academically exceptional as he is.

Jad and his family returned to Lebanon prior to July war of 2006. They returned because in Lebanon there is more emphasis on the community and on family support, which his parents believed to be very important, particularly in improving his social and emotional skills. Another reason for their return was that with the increased amount of assessments and studies and inspections done on their son, his parents could not help but be worried that they may lose him to the world of science and education. In Lebanon, his parents have noticed several changes in the way Jad was performing, both academically and socially. Jad had constantly complained that his school was too boring and not challenging enough for him, and did not take care of his specific needs and interests, such as in the areas of science, space, and astronomy. Jad was also being stigmatized as being a "nerd" or "weird" and had therefore tried to downplay his intelligence in order to fit in. At a certain point, his mother was upset to find out that he was performing rather poorly compared to his usual achievements because he "wanted to fit in" and did not want to show that his intelligence. After this discussion, Jad began to perform at his previously usual standard. Socially, Jad had some trouble adapting at first, particularly because many conversations and discussions in Lebanon revolve around politics and he did not enjoy that. However, as Jad's peers grew older, their topics of interest began to match more closely to what Jad was interested in and, therefore, made it more easy for him to relate. This was verified when he administered the WISC as part of Al-Hroub's study, and obtained a full IQ score of 116, which falls under the "Intellectually Average" range. It was later revealed that Jad was doing poorly on purpose to avoid being bullied. In order to overcome Jad's problem, Al-Hroub developed a program for gifted and talented, to be used at the school with Jad and other students. The program was developed to provide suitable services to accommodate Jad's intellectual, social, and emotional potential, but unfortunately, it was never implemented. When this issue was investigated, the results revealed that the school was not able to offer the program for administrative and financial reasons.

The authors of this book were motivated by Jad's story to write this book by exploring critical issues related to the conceptions, identification, characteristics, and programing for gifted and talented in Lebanese schools.

This book discusses research about gifted education in Lebanon and around the world, examining the latest theories on definitions and models of gifted education and different identification procedures of gifted students. It specifically addresses the problems faced in Lebanon in establishing a common definition and identification procedures. This book is written for researchers, professionals, and graduate students in the field of school psychology, educational psychology, and social work as well as teachers, counselors, policy-makers, principals, researchers, and specialists in gifted education.

Each chapter addresses the current status of gifted education in Lebanon explores contemporary definitions and theories of giftedness, and offers recommendations for future methods and practices to enhance gifted student learning. Chapter 1 provides a background on the status of gifted education in Lebanon and the challenges Lebanon faces with gifted education. Chapter 2 highlights recent and relevant international definitions of giftedness and sheds light on where Lebanon stands in relation to the world. In addition, misconceptions and underrepresentation of giftedness education are also explored. Chapter 3 focuses on current identification procedures used in discovering gifted students, providing background history as well as other tools currently used around the world. Chapter 4 discusses the research study and how it was conducted to address the two research questions aimed at exploring teachers' perception of giftedness in Lebanon and investigating the methods of identification that are currently used in schools. The findings of the research study are represented in Chapter 5, which discusses the teachers' perceptions in detail, along with secondary findings (e.g., gender identification and social giftedness). Chapter 6 concludes by synthesizing the different themes that arise from the teachers' discussions on giftedness and what factors constitute their perceptions of giftedness, and their need for training and awareness of giftedness. Furthermore, it addresses the implications of the research and offers recommendations made by the teachers in the study to benefit gifted students of Lebanon in the future.

Jounieh, Lebanon	Sara El Khoury
Beirut, Lebanon	Anies Al-Hroub

Contents

1 Introduction to Giftedness in Lebanon 1
2 Definitions and Conceptions of Giftedness Around the World 9
3 Identification of Gifted Students: History, Tools, and Procedures ... 39
4 Researching Teachers' Perceptions and Procedures
   for Identification of Giftedness in Lebanon 61
5 Defining and Identifying Giftedness in Lebanon: Findings
   from the Field 73
6 Giftedness in Lebanon: Emerging Issues and Future
   Considerations 95

Appendix A: Perceptions of Giftedness Survey 111

Appendix B: Protocol of Focus Group Discussion with Teachers 115

Appendix C: Teacher Interview Protocol 117

Index 119

About the Authors

Sara El Khoury is the Program Coordinator of USP VI, USAID, in the American University of Beirut (AUB), which helps Lebanese underprivileged students attain a USAID scholarship at AUB. Ms. Khoury previously worked in Adma International School as a special needs teacher, where she taught students with severe learning disabilities, including down syndrome, cognitive delay, autism, dyslexia, and gifted students in middle school. She created and implemented curricula that were approved and used in the school. Ms. Khoury completed her MA in Educational Psychology (with emphasis on School Guidance and Counseling), BA in Elementary Education (with emphasis on English and Social Studies Education), and a teaching diploma in Special Education from the American University of Beirut (AUB). Ms. Khoury was also a research associate on a project funded by the Welfare Association regarding different aspects of education in the Palestinian camps in Lebanon.

Anies Al-Hroub is the Chairperson of the Department of Education at the American University of Beirut. He is an Associate Professor of Education Psychology and Special Education and the coordinator of the Special Education program. Al-Hroub completed his PhD and MPhil in Special Education (Giftedness and Learning Disabilities) from the University of Cambridge and his MA (Special Education) and BA (Psychology) from the University of Jordan. He also obtained a Higher Diploma in "Learning Disabilities" from Balka Applied University. He was selected as the British Academy Visiting Scholar to the Faculty of Education at the University of Cambridge in 2010, and a Visiting Scholar to the School of Advanced Social Studies (SASS) in Slovenia. His publications appeared in leading international gifted and special education journals in addition to two published books entitled, *Theories and Programs of Education for the Gifted and Talented* (1999), and *ADHD in Lebanese Schools: Diagnosis, Assessment and Treatment* (spring 2016). His research interests focus on gifted and talented education, learning disabilities, dyslexia, twice-exceptionality, early childhood education, educational assessment, psychometric and dynamic assessment, guidance and counseling, metacognition, and school dropout. He has led several educational projects sponsored by UNICEF, UNRWA, the British Academy, USAID, Issam Fares Institute for Public Policy and International Affairs (IFI), and Welfare Association and served as consultant for UNESCO, the Asfari Foundation, and the Center for Civic Engagement and Community Service (CCECS) at AUB.

List of Abbreviations

ACGT	Arab Council for Gifted and Talented
AUB	American University of Beirut
CAB	Clinical Assessment of Behavior
ENTER	Explore, Narrow, Test, Evaluate, and Review
FGD	Focus Group Discussion
GCSE	General Certificate in Secondary Education
GRS	Gifted Rating Scales
IB	International Baccalaureate
ICIE	International Center for Excellence and Innovation
IEP	Individualized Education Plan
IHW	Iranian Hierarchical Wisdom model
IQ	Intelligence Quotient
LAU	Lebanese American University
MEHE	Ministry of Education and Higher Education
MI	Multiple Intelligences
MMG	Munich Model of Giftedness
NCERD	National Center for Educational Research and Development
NDU	Notre Dame University–Louaize
NGO	Non-Governmental Organizations
SAT	Scholastic Aptitude Test or Scholastic Assessment Test
SRBCSS	Scales for Rating the Behavioral Characteristics of Superior Students
WCGTC	World Council for Gifted and Talented Children
WICS	Wisdom, Intelligence, and Creativity Synthesized

List of Figures

Fig. 5.1	Bar graph illustrates teachers' perceptions of gifted students' mathematical skills..	77
Fig. 5.2	Bar graph illustrates teachers' perceptions of gifted students having high social intelligence...	80
Fig. 5.3	Bar graph illustrates responses for leadership and communication skills	81
Fig. 5.4	Bar graph illustrates teachers' perceptions of gifted students taking the lead in small groups	82
Fig. 5.5	Bar graph illustrates teachers' perceptions of gifted students' creative abilities to solve problems...	82
Fig. 5.6	Bar graph illustrates teachers' perceptions of gifted students' ability to produce solutions...	83
Fig. 5.7	Bar graph illustrates teachers' perceptions of gifted students' speediness in completing assignments...	85
Fig. 5.8	Bar graph illustrates teachers' perceptions of gifted students' ability to learn easily and quickly	86
Fig. 5.9	Bar graph illustrates teachers' perceptions on gifted students as having a large amount of general knowledge	88
Fig. 5.10	Bar graph illustrates teachers' perceptions of behavioral characteristics..	90
Figs. 5.11 and 5.12.	Bar graphs illustrating the perception that boys have higher mathematical/logical abilities; perception that girls have higher verbal abilities...	93

List of Tables

Table 4.1	Composition of sample by gender and school	63
Table 5.1	Teachers' perceptions of the importance of mathematical skills	78
Table 5.2	Teachers' perceptions of social intelligence	80
Table 5.3	Teachers' perceptions of leadership and communication skills	81
Table 5.4	Teachers' perceptions of leadership and communication skills – continued	82
Table 5.5	Teachers' perceptions of creativity and solving problems	83
Table 5.6	Teachers' perceptions of responses to finding solutions	84
Table 5.7	Teachers' perceptions of speediness in completing assignments	85
Table 5.8	Teachers' perceptions about absorbing information rapidly	86
Table 5.9	Teachers' perceptions of general knowledge	87
Table 5.10	Teachers' perceptions of behavioral characteristics	90
Table 5.11	Teacher's perceptions of gender differentiation (all figures are in %)	93

Chapter 1
Introduction to Giftedness in Lebanon

Anies Al-Hroub and Sara El Khoury

Abstract This chapter provides the background to the research and practices regarding giftedness in Lebanon. Consequently, this chapter will present the current definitions of giftedness according to research and theory and will shed light on existing identification practices and programs used in Lebanon as reported in the research. It will discuss the status of gifted education in Lebanon, existing challenges, and future opportunities.

1.1 Introduction

Differing definitions of giftedness and diverse procedures for identifying gifted students have been a constant problem in the field, with consequent difficulties when it comes to identifying, placing, and providing appropriate services for students who are gifted (Al-Hroub, 2010a, 2010b, 2012, 2013, 2014b, 2016; Bracken & Brown, 2006).

1.2 Gifted Education in Lebanon

Lebanon lacks a formal system of education for gifted students, because the emphasis in the national school curriculum remains on mainstream education, which is the case in most Arab countries. However, in Beirut, the capital city of

---

Anies Al-Hroub (✉)
Department of Education, Chairperson, American University of Beirut, Beirut, Lebanon
e-mail: aa111@aub.edu.lb

Sara El Khoury
Department of Education, American University of Beirut, Jounieh, Lebanon
e-mail: sie07@aub.edu.lb

© The Author(s), under exclusive licence to Springer International Publishing
AG, part of Springer Nature 2018
S. El Khoury, A. Al-Hroub, *Gifted Education in Lebanese Schools*,
SpringerBriefs in Psychology, https://doi.org/10.1007/978-3-319-78592-9_1

Lebanon, some private schools cater for high-achieving students. Although these private schools do offer some enrichment programs, they are often limited in content and scope especially when compared to enrichment programs being offered in schools abroad such as North America and Europe (Al-Hroub, 2016; Sarouphim, 2009). Sarouphim (2010) believes that the lack of understanding of the construct of giftedness is the main reason for the shortage of gifted education in Lebanon. She also states that Lebanon lacks the appropriate means, assessment, and procedures to identify gifted students. Similarly, Diab (2006) affirms:

> The only tests used to assess intelligence in Lebanon are imported from the West (mostly France and the United States) and translated into Arabic, the native language of the Lebanese. On occasion, these tests are administered in English or French, as most Lebanese students are fluent in at least one of these two foreign languages. (p. 81)

According to Al-Hroub (2013, 2014b, 2016), these tests provide only an estimate of the students' intellectual ability, and IQ tests cannot be the sole measure for giftedness. Consequently, there is a need for the provision of more reliable and valid identification methods in addition to programs suited for gifted students.

There is one advantage to the current lack of gifted programs in Lebanon, according to Sarouphim (2009). She labels this advantage the "clean slate" phenomenon, stating that "educators can start working afresh, moulding the field of education of the gifted based on empirical evidence yielded by the pool of research findings already available in the Western literature, a process potentially less problematic than attempting to fix flaws in pre-existing programs" (p. 277). What this comes down to is that using Western studies can help tremendously with gifted research in Lebanon; however, educators should take caution, as they cannot blindly replicate Western evidence to the Lebanese context. Therefore, the first mode of action is to view and explore the current perceptions of teachers on giftedness to see how wide the gap is between on-the-ground application and knowledge of giftedness and current research. How much of the research is being applied?

It should be noted that all schools in Lebanon, whether public or private, must follow a national curriculum mandated by the Ministry of Education and Higher Education (MEHE). Catering for students with special needs was made compulsory in the latest revision of this curriculum (NCERD, 1995). The provisions in the most recent version require offering support services and remedial classes to students with learning disabilities but leave out any references to services of any kind intended for gifted students. The only thing that the Lebanese law provides for gifted students is grade-based acceleration, where there is a possibility for the gifted learner to skip one grade level in cycle one (grades 1, 2, 3) and another in cycle two (grades 4, 5, 6). This means that a gifted 11-year-old student could potentially reach grade 8 if he/she were to skip one grade in cycle one and another in cycle two (Chaar, 2016).

The Lebanese Parliament in May 2000 approved Public Law 220, which provides a legislative framework for the education of people with disabilities (Wehbi, 2006), and Article 59 of this Law "guarantees the right to equal educational and learning opportunities for all people with disabilities" (Wehbi, 2006, p. 323).

Furthermore, Article 60 declares, "a disability should not restrict access to any educational institution or setting in Lebanon" (Sarouphim, 2010, p. 72). Again, there is no reference to the education of gifted students. The scope of special education in Lebanon is limited to students with disabilities, as there is no mention of gifted education within Lebanese law or in the revised national curriculum. Sarouphim (2010, 2015) points out that when it comes to educating the gifted in Lebanon, it has not been a matter of encouraging gifted education or discouraging it but simply ignoring it.

1.3 Existing Challenges to Gifted and Talented Education in Lebanon and Future Opportunities

Al-Hroub (2016) identified seven main challenges to gifted and talented education in Lebanon: (1) the Ministry of Education and Higher Education (MEHE) has no educational policy for gifted education in Lebanon; (2) there is a lack of understanding of the very concept of giftedness in Lebanese schools and educational institutions; (3) there is a lack of valid and reliable tools in Arabic for the identification of gifted and talented children; (4) several groups of gifted children are neglected and marginalized, such as twice-exceptional children (i.e., gifted with learning disabilities, gifted with autism, gifted but underachieving, and female gifted learners); (5) there is a lack of preservice academic programs on gifted and talented education in Lebanese universities; (6) there are no, or poor, services and facilities for gifted and talented children at Lebanese schools; and (7) most nongovernmental organizations (NGOs) are interested in sponsoring special education projects that focus on the education of children with disabilities but neither for educational projects regarding the intellectually gifted nor those having special talents.

Despite these challenges and the lack of formal programs and services that cater for gifted students, Al-Hroub (2016) identified three main future opportunities for promoting gifted and talented education in Lebanon: first, the increasing number of research projects on issues related to the identification and teaching of gifted and talented children; second, the increasing collaboration with regional and international associations concerned with gifted learners (e.g., the World Council for Gifted and Talented Children [WCGTC], the International Centre for Innovation in Education [ICIE], and the Arab Council for the Gifted and Talented [ACGT]); and finally, a number of Lebanese universities which have already started addressing the aforementioned challenges by introducing new courses, tracks, or academic programs that focus on gifted education. The American University of Beirut (AUB) already offers a diploma for special needs. However, during the academic year of 2012–2013, the education department restructured its special education program and offered a new area of concentration in gifted and talented education. Thus, the focus in AUB is shifting away from students with disabilities and more toward students with gifts and talents. The learning outcomes of the gifted and talented program are to (a) apply the pedagogical and instructional strategies to work with children and youth who exhibit learning disabilities and/or gifts and talents; (b) integrate theory, research, and practice to inform decisions in special educational settings; (c) use communication, collaboration, and consultation skills to work with children, youth, families, related service personnel, school-based teachers, and community agencies; (d) design quality programs needed to work with children, youth, families, related service personnel, school-based teachers, and community agencies; (e) identify gifted and talented students; (f) design individualized educational programs for gifted and talented students; (g) modify instruction and curricula for students with gifts and talents; and (h) use assistive technology, instructional support, and accommodations to support inclusive learning environments (Department of Education, 2013).

The Lebanese American University (LAU) also offers a diploma in gifted education and one in learning disabilities, separate from the bachelor's degree. It is comprised of 21 credits and requires a full year's study to obtain. The learning outcomes that are expected of students who pursue the diploma in learning disabilities or gifted education are as follows: (1) actively implement effective evidence-based instructional strategies, (2) apply scientifically based methodology to improve interventions for gifted students, (3) advocate for and safeguard the human and civil rights of individuals with exceptionalities and their families, (4) identify and apply effective instructional practices for the education of gifted students, (5) evaluate progress of students using valid tools toward Individualized Education Plan (IEP) goals, and finally (6) apply instructional materials and evaluation tools within a multilingual context (LAU catalog, 2016).

Other universities such as Notre Dame University – Louaize (NDU) offer gifted education courses as an option toward fulfilling one of the major requirements to obtain an undergraduate degree in education. The course requirements, along with their respective percentages, are divided into four sections: (1) General Education Requirements (31%); (2) Core Requirements (23%); (3) Major Requirements in Early Childhood, Learning Disabilities or Education of the Gifted (40%); and (4) Free Electives (6%). Education of the gifted is given as one choice out of three other specialties, and it is not a requirement for obtaining a BA in Education (Al-Hroub, 2014a).

Most of these programs are relatively new, so it will take some time for Lebanese teachers who graduate with a Gifted Education diploma to coordinate the meager and inconsistent resources that already exist, with the necessary additional resources that will need to be introduced, in order to appropriately identify students who are gifted and to consequently offer the appropriate support.

1.4 Research Aims and Questions

In Lebanon, little research has been done on gifted learners and gifted education (Al-Hroub, 2016). In order to develop programs in gifted education that have solid foundations, there is a need for research on existing conceptions regarding giftedness, the prevailing identification procedures, and whether either is founded on evidenced-based definitions of giftedness. Therefore, the purpose of this study was to investigate and explore the current understanding and conception of giftedness that is prevalent among teachers in Lebanon in order to construct a baseline, to compose an existing definition, and to ascertain the current identification procedures that are offered to gifted students. Hence, our aims were twofold: (a) to explore the perceptions teachers currently have concerning the attributes of gifted students and (b) to survey the current practices of identifying gifted students. Therefore, the research questions guiding this study were: (a) What are Lebanese private, elementary school teachers' conceptions of the attributes of gifted students? (b) What are the current practices used to identify gifted students?

1.5 Rationale

Whether a student has been identified or is believed to be gifted, his or her education becomes the most important priority in order to maintain his/her attention, to enrich his/her fields of interest, and finally to motivate and challenge him/her to reach his/her utmost potential. In Lebanon, according to Al-Hroub (2016) and Sarouphim (2015), a growing interest in the education of the gifted has been noted among educators and scholars even though, at present, the country lacks a formal system for educating these students. For this reason, identification procedures present a major issue. In order to develop programs in gifted education that are built on empirical evidence, the country is in need for research on identification measures, given that the growing interest in this field will eventually lead to the establishment of programs for the gifted in Lebanese schools.

Before there can even be talk about establishing gifted education programs, the definition of what it means to be gifted must be agreed upon. There should be a consensus in order to develop sound identification procedures and programs to ensure that the gifted students are being correctly identified and accordingly receive the education that they deserve. There exists a gap in the literature as very little research can be found on procedures for identifying gifted students in Lebanon and on how Lebanon currently defines giftedness. This is the first study in Lebanon that explores the existing cultural definition of giftedness in Lebanese schools. This study was designed to reveal where the gap fell between the current, disparate, individual perceptions of giftedness and whatever informed, authoritative, and official working definition of giftedness might be adopted. We focused on the scope of teachers' conceptions of giftedness without any preconceived notions due to a complete lack of any previous studies on this subject in Lebanon. Because no studies have been conducted regarding teachers' conceptions of giftedness, we set out to explore issue with Lebanese teachers.

We chose to include elementary teachers for our study. The reason that we decided to include elementary teachers in our study was that, as Silverman (2007) states, "the ideal time frame for testing for giftedness is between the ages of 5 and 8 years. After 9 years of age, gifted children may hit the ceiling of tests, and gifted girls may [already] be socialized to hide their abilities" (Silverman, 2007, p. 27). We believe that early identification is essential because it leads to early intervention, and this promotes the optimal development of gifted students.

The mixed method approach has been adopted in this study, because the use of surveys would not have sufficed: the best method for exploring perceptions is through qualitative research techniques, such as interviews and focus group discussions. A qualitative research design was deemed to be the most appropriate because of its focus on revealing individual understandings or conceptions (Lee, 2006); otherwise, the study would have been incomplete.

1.6 Significance of the Study

This study has theoretical and practical implications. The theoretical implication involves the distillation of a dynamic definition of giftedness, which combines the current beliefs that Lebanese teachers and stakeholders have on gifted education. In this study, we gathered teachers' perceptions of giftedness and combined them to devise the prevailing general definition of giftedness: to discover what is currently on the ground in Lebanon. It has been the intention following this study to formulate one consistent, informed, official definition of giftedness for all of Lebanon to use. As long as there is no clear, consistent definition of giftedness that still exists, then it is, and will remain, impossible to generate programs for the gifted population.

The practical solution will be to construct a common definition of giftedness in Lebanon to eliminate the frequency of misconceptions. In addition, viewing and exploring the current teachers' perceptions on giftedness would help us examine how wide the gap is between on-the-ground application and teachers' knowledge of giftedness. Much current research in the field is missing or sporadic as well. How much of the research is being applied? Most importantly, any practices that are being implemented should be built on solid-based theory and evidence. A unified Lebanon policy would meet the needs of gifted students much better than if each school were to act on its own. Lebanon is a country with a long history of conflict; it would be very beneficial to recognize the talents of gifted students and nurture their minds since they may provide finally the promise of a much better future for Lebanon.

References

Al-Hroub, A. (2010a). Developing assessment profiles for mathematically gifted children with learning difficulties in England. *Journal of Education for the Gifted, 34*(1), 7–44.
Al-Hroub, A. (2010b). Programming for mathematically gifted children with learning difficulties in Jordan. *Roeper Review, 32*, 259–271.
Al-Hroub, A. (2012). Theoretical issues surrounding the concept of gifted with learning difficulties. *International Journal for Research in Education, 31*, 30–60.

References

Al-Hroub, A. (2013). Multidimensional model for the identification of gifted children with learning disabilities. *Gifted and Talented International, 28*, 51–69.

Al-Hroub, A. (2014a). Quality issues in education programs in the Arab universities: A Synthesis study. قضايا النوعية في برامج التربية في الجامعات العربية. In A. Amine (Ed.), *Quality issues in higher education in the Arab countries* (pp. 55–76). Beirut: The Lebanese Association for Educational Studies.

Al-Hroub, A. (2014b). Identification of dual-exceptional learners. *Procedia-Social and Behavioral Science Journal, 116*, 63–73.

Al-Hroub, A. (2016). *Challenges to gifted and talented education in Lebanon. Seminar on the status of gifted education in Lebanon: Challenges and future opportunities*. American University of Beirut. The Arab Council for Gifted and Talented in Lebanon.

Bracken, B. A., & Brown, E. F. (2006). Behavioral identification and assessment of gifted and talented students. *Journal of Psychoeducational Assessment, 24*(2), 112–122.

Chaar, R. (2016). *Educators' unawareness of the needs of the gifted students and its effect on their learning and productivity in schools of Beirut* (Unpublished MA thesis). International Lebanese University, Lebanon.

Department of Education. (2013). *The Department of Education program review: A self-study report 2013–2014*. Beirut, Lebanon: American University of Beirut.

Diab, R. (2006). University students' beliefs about learning English and French in Lebanon. *System, 34*(1), 80–96.

LAU Catalog. (2016). *Diploma in learning disabilities and giftedness*. Lebanon: Lebanese American University (LAU).

Lee, L. (2006). Teachers' conceptions of gifted and talented young children. *High Ability Studies, 10*(2), 183–196.

National Center for Educational Research and Development (NCERD). (1995). *Lebanese national curriculum*. Beirut: Lebanon.

Sarouphim, K. M. (2009). The use of a performance assessment for identifying gifted Lebanese students: Is DISCOVER effective? *Journal for the Education of the Gifted, 33*(2), 275–295.

Sarouphim, K. M. (2010). A model for the education of gifted learners in Lebanon. *International Journal of Special Education, 25*(1), 71–79.

Sarouphim, K. M. (2015). Slowly but surely: Small steps towards establishing gifted education programs in Lebanon. *Journal for the Education of the Gifted, 38*(2), 196–211.

Silverman, L. K. (2007). *What we learned about gifted children 1979–2007*. Gifted Development Centre: Denver, CO..

Wehbi, S. (2006). The challenges of inclusive education in Lebanon. *Disability & Society, 21*(4), 331–343.

Chapter 2
Definitions and Conceptions of Giftedness Around the World

Anies Al-Hroub and Sara El Khoury

Abstract This chapter presents a critical review on the international definitions of giftedness and teachers' perceptions of giftedness around the world, in order to have a better understanding and assessment of where Lebanon stands. This chapter also sheds light on how different cultures perceive giftedness. Moreover, misconceptions and misdiagnoses of gifted children are explored, along with stereotypes that are popular around the world.

2.1 Introduction

The abundance of diverse definitions of giftedness and different identification methods has become a major problem. Because there is a substantial amount of differing identification methods and definitions, this leads to problems in identifying, referring, and providing appropriate services to students who are gifted (Al-Hroub, 2010a, 2010b, 2012, 2013, 2014; Bracken & Brown, 2006).

2.2 Problems with Defining Giftedness and its Consequences

Finding and agreeing on a definition is difficult for two reasons. According to Renzulli (1979), the first reason is that a definition can "limit or restrict the number of performance areas that are considered in determining the eligibility for special programs (p. 180)". A "conservative" definition might actually limit a student from

---

Anies Al-Hroub (✉)
Department of Education, Chairperson, American University of Beirut, Beirut, Lebanon
e-mail: aa111@aub.edu.lb

Sara El Khoury
Department of Education, American University of Beirut, Jounieh, Lebanon
e-mail: sie07@aub.edu.lb

© The Author(s), under exclusive licence to Springer International Publishing AG, part of Springer Nature 2018
S. El Khoury, A. Al-Hroub, *Gifted Education in Lebanese Schools*,
SpringerBriefs in Psychology, https://doi.org/10.1007/978-3-319-78592-9_2

entering a gifted program purely because the program might consider academic performance only and exclude other areas such as art, drama, music, leadership, public speaking, and creative writing. Renzulli's second stated reason for finding and agreeing on a definition is that "a definition may specify the degree or level of excellence one must attain to be considered gifted" (p. 180). What's more, the definition of what constitutes whether a student is gifted has changed significantly over the years. However, it is not only these three misalignments that create problems. The very notion of giftedness varies from culture to culture; consequently, the inception of gifted research varies as well.

2.3 Approach to Giftedness Research

According to Ziegler and Raul (2000) and in line with the philosopher Auguste Comte (1798–1857), the approach to giftedness research has progressed mainly through three stages: theological, metaphysical, and empirical. The theological approach refers to individuals having a higher power or being seen as supernatural beings. This can be seen in different cultures; for example, both Plato in Greece and Confucius in China refer to "heavenly children." Similarly, the Bible refers to "Having then gifts differing according to the grace that is given to us" (Romans 12:6, King James Version, as cited in Robinson & Clinkenbeard, 2008). The next phase, the metaphysical stage, refers to giftedness as being associated more with the human individual and less with the supernatural being. During this period, some gifted qualities resembled that of a "crazed genius"; the more gifted you were, the more insane or crazy you were likely to be. Moreover, it was also more likely that these highly gifted individuals were prone to having mental illnesses. These "crazed geniuses" were therefore often thought of as problematic, which to some extent is still applicable today. However, beginning in the twentieth century, the third period – the empirical stage – became more popular in defining gifted students. Defining and identifying gifted students in the empirical stage meant relying more on scientific methods and research, and they were able to actually measure intelligence using different scales (Sternberg & Davidson, 2005).

2.4 Definitions of Giftedness

Differing definitions of giftedness and diverse procedures for identifying gifted students have been a constant problem in the field, with consequent difficulties when it comes to identifying, placing, and providing appropriate services for students who are gifted (Al-Hroub, 2010a, 2010b, 2012, 2013, 2014b; Bracken & Brown, 2006). In 1972, a committee was formed by the United States. Commissioner of Education (Marland Jr., 1972) proposed a definition of giftedness that included performance domains as well as academic domains. Other contemporary definitions arise from Marland:

2.4 Definitions of Giftedness

> Gifted and Talented children are those identified by professionally qualified persons, who by virtue of outstanding abilities are capable of high performance. These are children who require differentiated educational programs and services beyond those normally provided by the regular school program in order to realise their contributions to self and society. Children capable of high performance include those with demonstrated achievement and/or potential ability in any of the following areas: (a) general intellectual ability; (b) specific academic aptitude; (c) creative or productive thinking; (d) leadership ability and; (e) visual and performing arts. (Marland Jr., 1972, p. 2)

Modern conceptions of giftedness are the result of an evolution of ideas. Each generation of gifted theories has built upon the one before it, thus integrating previous iterations and research while adding components reflecting the current state of research (Kaufman & Sternberg, 2008). An early and still common definition of giftedness was on top scores obtained in standardized IQ tests. Alfred Binet created the first IQ test in 1905 in order to predict success in school, not as a measure of innate intelligence or "raw" genetically based potential (Gardner, 1992). Unfortunately, many researchers, psychologists, educators, and people in general have believed that IQ scores are a major factor in determining and measuring intelligence and giftedness (Sarouphim, 1999). Opponents of this view believe that such scores do not provide sufficient evidence to decide whether a student is gifted or not. They argue that the IQ test is limited by only testing linguistic and logical-mathematical abilities leaving out other important abilities such as spatial, personal, musical, and artistic skills (Gardner, 1992). IQ tests exclude other significant factors, such as motivation, effort, and creativity, which are key components of more recent definitions of giftedness. Another reason for dissatisfaction of IQ testing as a sole identification method is that its use has led to major underrepresentation of students coming from culturally diverse and economically disadvantaged groups (Callahan, 2005). This may be due to the IQ tests' overreliance on verbal skills, in which minority students often lag behind (Sarouphim, 2009).

In 1977, Renzulli reconceptualized a definition of giftedness, referring to it as the three-ring model. He hypothesized that giftedness is an interaction between three clusters of basic traits: above-average general ability, high levels of creativity, and high levels of motivation (task commitment). Similarly, in 1993, Maker proposed that creativity and intelligence can be interlinked; for example, she affirmed that "creative problem-solving" is a characteristic of giftedness. In late 1996, she stated that the key element in identifying gifted students is the ability to solve complex problems in the "most efficient, effective, or economical ways" (p. 44).

Renzulli described what each ability means; above-average ability (high ability) was defined, according to Renzulli, as having high levels of verbal and numerical reasoning, abstract thinking, spatial relations, memory, and fluency. He also mentioned "automatization" of information processing, which referred to rapid, accurate, and selective retrieval of information. He went on to describe another factor in high-level thinking, specific ability. He defined specific ability as "the application of various combinations of the above general abilities to one or more specialized areas of knowledge or areas of human performance (e.g. the arts, leadership, [and] administration)" (p. 9). In other words, a gifted student is one who is able to acquire and make use of vast amounts of information and to simultaneously apply their skills to particular problems or manifest them in their specialized areas of performance. Additionally they have the skills to sort out relevant and irrelevant information when solving a particular problem.

Moving on to the ability of task commitment, Renzulli defined it as "the capacity for high levels of interest, enthusiasm, and involvement in a particular problem, area of study, or form of human expression" (p. 9). "Task commitment" is the ability to commit, to have perseverance and determination, and to be completely dedicated to the task they are doing. The student presents a large amount of self-confidence, a strong ego and a belief in his/her ability to carry out important work, freedom from inferiority feelings, and a drive to achieve. This also includes setting high standards for his/her work and being able to maintain openness to self and external criticism.

Finally, Renzulli explained creativity as having fluency, flexibility, and originality of thought. In other words, the student would be open to new experiences and receptive to new ideas, no matter how bizarre or different. These students are usually very curious, speculative, and adventurous and are willing to take risks in thought and action. They are also very sensitive to detail and are able to act on and react to external stimulation and one's own ideas and feelings (Renzulli, 1986).

When a number of traits are presented, as with Renzulli, there tend to be an overlap with individual items and an interaction between and among the general categories and the specific traits (Renzulli, 1986). However, Renzulli clearly pointed out that not all the traits have to be present in a single individual for that person to be designated as gifted. As the model name (three-ring conception of giftedness) emphasizes, there is an interaction among the three clusters, rather than a single cluster. Renzulli's model is very important because it recognizes nonintellectual traits, such as task commitment, not only intellectual traits. However, one of its major shortcomings is that it does not allow the identification of an underachieving student as being gifted, because some students may have plenty of intellectual ability and creativity but lack motivation and task commitment (Lee Corbin & Denicolo, 1998; Rimm, Siegle, & Davis, 2018).

On the other hand, Tannenbaum (1979) believed that children could be *potentially* gifted if these eight types of developed talent (which are rarely demonstrated in childhood) are nurtured. Tannenbaum proposed three questions in order to predict the child's *promise* of giftedness, especially when combined with a particular maturity, which is often found in adulthood. The three questions are: "(1) Who qualifies to join the pool of possibly gifted individuals? (2) What broad realms of achievement among pool members are judged for signs of excellence? (3) How do pool members demonstrate their giftedness in these domains of human accomplishment?" (Colangelo & Davis, 2003, p. 45). In order to answer the "who" question, Tannenbaum explained that there are two types of gifted people: producers and performers. What do producers produce? Thoughts and tangibles. What do performers perform? Staged artistry and human services. How do all the above produce their excellence? By working creatively and proficiently.

Thus, the following eight groups of individuals that stem from the three questions are (1) the producer of creative thoughts (philosophers, novelists, dramatists, and the theoretical or experimental scientist); (2) the producer of proficient thoughts, mean-

2.4 Definitions of Giftedness

ing one who can solve complex problems such as math and science while having deep insights; (3) the creative producer of tangibles (the inventor of scientific technology that is able to create patent products, architects, and sculptors); (4) the proficient producer of tangibles (the worker who puts more effort in being meticulous, rather than original, such as diamond polishers, craftsmen who produce traditional furniture faithfully, and toolmakers who work by hand); (5) the creative performer of staged artistry (interpreters and recreators); (6) the proficient performer of staged artistry (dancers who stay true to the choreographer's art and orchestral musicians); (7) the creative performer of human services (innovative teachers and social workers); and finally (8) the proficient performer of human services (classroom teachers who follow the guidelines very carefully and diagnosticians). There are many more examples; however these few have been included for the purposes of providing an overview.

Tannenbaum (1979) then produced the Star Model, where five elements mesh and contribute to gifted behavior. The five elements are (1) general ability, (2) special aptitude, (3) non-intellective requisites, (4) environmental supports, and (5) chance. These five elements combined illustrate the gifted child.

In 1983, Gardner (2011) was opposed to the severe limitations of the IQ test scores in assessing giftedness, as they undervalue students' other strengths. Gardner argued that gifted students needed to have a more well-rounded education and that teachers should reach all students, not only those who excel in logical and linguistic intelligences (Al-Hroub, 2009). In his theory of multiple intelligences (1983), Gardner described seven types of intelligences, later adding an eighth (naturalist intelligence) in 1996. The following is a list of all eight of Gardner's original eight intelligences: (1) linguistic (verbal) intelligence, which includes verbal comprehension, syntax, semantics, and written and oral expression; (2) logical-mathematical intelligence, which includes inductive and deductive reasoning; (3) spatial intelligence, which is the capacity to represent and manipulate three-dimensional configurations; (4) musical intelligence, which includes pitch discrimination, sensitivity to rhyme, texture, and timbre; (5) bodily-kinesthetic intelligence, which is the ability to use all or part of one's body to perform a task; (6) interpersonal intelligence, which is the ability to understand actions and motivations of others and act sensibly based on that knowledge; (7) intrapersonal intelligence, which is a person's understanding of one's own cognition, strengths and weaknesses, thinking styles, feelings, and emotions; and Gardner's later addition to these intelligences, which he called (8) naturalist intelligence, which is a spiritual, moral, existential, and naturalist intelligence (Gardner, 2011). The main criticism with Gardner's theory is the difficulty in identifying the separate intelligences (Clark, 2013).

Sternberg's (1985) triarchic theory of intelligence, like Gardner's (1983) theory of multiple intelligences, is a comprehensive, flexible, and inclusive theory, which contends, "Giftedness is a social construct that manifests itself in many ways and means different things to different cultural groups. Both Gardner and Sternberg acknowledged the multifaceted, complex nature of intelligence and how current tests (which are too simplistic and static) fail to do justice to this construct" (Colangelo & Davis, 2003, p. 514). Sternberg identified three main types of intelligence: (1) Analytical giftedness "is the academic talent measured by typical intelligence tests, particularly analytical reasoning and reading comprehension; (2)

Synthetic giftedness refers to creativity, insightfulness, intuition, or the ability to cope with novelty. Such persons may not earn the highest IQ, but ultimately they make the greatest contribution to society; and (3) Practical giftedness involves applying analytic and/or synthetic abilities successfully to everyday, pragmatic situations" (Sternberg, 2004, p. 326). Sternberg went on to state that the central aspect of giftedness is being able to coordinate the three abilities, knowing when to use which one, and having a balance between the three. He used the term "mental manager" to describe this phenomenon. In 2000, Sternberg had modified his triarchic theory to include wisdom as a subtype of practical intelligence. Wisdom, according to Sternberg, centers on the concern for "the needs and welfare of others" (Sternberg, 2000, p. 61). Therefore, "high wisdom" means giving good advice to others as well as to oneself. Sternberg came up with a new model of giftedness, called the WICS model of giftedness. Giftedness in this model is perceived as a synthesis of wisdom, intelligence, and creativity (Sternberg, 2004). The WICS model stipulates that:

> ...in life, people need creative skills and attitudes to produce new and original ideas; analytical skills and attitudes (academic intelligence) to evaluate the quality of these ideas; practical skills and attitudes (practical intelligence) to execute ideas and to persuade others of their value; and wisdom-related skills and attitudes in order to ensure that one's ideas help to foster a common good, rather than only the good of oneself and those closely associated with oneself. Gifted people, in this view, are not necessarily extremely strong in all of these aspects. Rather, they recognize and capitalize on their strengths, and recognize and compensate for or correct their weaknesses, in order to adapt to, shape, and select real-world environments. (p. 331)

Sternberg later expanded his triarchic/WICS theory, which eventually evolved into the theory of successful intelligence which states:

> People are successfully intelligent to the extent that they have the abilities needed to succeed in life, according to their own definition of success within their sociocultural context. They succeed by adapting to, shaping, and selecting environments, which they do by recognizing and then capitalizing on their strengths, and by recognizing and then compensating for or correcting their weaknesses. (p. 43)

In their critique, Kaufman and Sternberg (2008) also established that conceptions of giftedness often change over time. Sternberg argued that the four attributes (analytical, synthetic, and practical giftedness and wisdom) are not fixed and that they can be modified and nurtured over time (Sternberg, 2004). Kaufman and Sternberg gave the example of how in the past, a student's ability to learn classical Greek and Latin quickly was a sign of giftedness, but nowadays, this ability is less valued. They also pointed out that conceptions of giftedness are usually based on either explicit or implicit theories of giftedness. They explained this explicitly as follows:

> An explicit theory is one proposed by a scientist or educator who has studied giftedness and has arrived at a conception of giftedness that has been subject to some kind of empirical test. An implicit theory is simply a layperson's conception of a phenomenon. It has no explicit scientific basis. It might be looked upon as a "pragmatic" conception rather than one based on rigorous research. (p. 72)

In the same way as Gardner's theory, Sternberg's model was also criticized for being too complex to be tested in any appreciatively specific manner.

However, in 1991, a group of theorists, practitioners, psychologists, and parents set out to form a new definition for giftedness that included more than just certain behaviors, achievement, school placements, and other factors. They believed that these elements missed the essence of giftedness. They then formed the following definition:

> Giftedness is asynchronous development in which advanced cognitive abilities and heightened intensity combine to create inner experiences and awareness that are qualitatively different from the norm. This asynchrony increases with higher intellectual capacity. The uniqueness of the gifted renders them particularly vulnerable and requires modifications in parenting, teaching, and counseling in order for them to develop optimally. (The Columbus Group, 1991, as cited in Morelock, 1992, p. 14)

According to Silverman (1993b), the Columbus definition entailed that gifted children develop in an uneven manner; as they are more complex than comparable children in their age groups are, they feel out of place. The higher the child's IQ, the higher the discrepancies are, leaving the gifted child more vulnerable.

Unlike Renzulli, Gagné drew a distinction between intellectual and creative ability (Al-Hroub, 2009). He emphasized that is it not necessary for a student to have high potential in both intellect and creativity before they can be acknowledged as gifted. Gagné's Differentiated Model of Giftedness and Talent was therefore another paradigm developed in order to identify giftedness in students. Gagné distinguished between giftedness and talent and defined giftedness as "the possession and use of untrained and spontaneously expressed natural abilities in at least one domain, to a degree that places a child at least among the top 10% of his or her age peers" (2004, p. 60). On the other hand, he defined talent as "the superior mastery of systematically developed abilities (or skills) in at least one field of human activity to a degree that places a child's achievement within the upper 10% of age peers who are active in the field" (2004, p. 60). In this model, giftedness includes four aptitude domains: intellectual, creative, socioaffective, and sensorimotor (Gagné, 2004). Moreover, unlike Renzulli's theory, Munro (2002) suggested that Gagné's model would be able to identify students with high ability but who at the same time might be underachieving due to demotivation or environmental factors.

Finally, Gottfredson (2003) described a three-level, pyramid-shaped model of intelligence. At the top of the pyramid is the (1) basic intelligence or g. The middle level (2) consists of general abilities, which are correlated to the g. Finally, the bottom tier (3) includes myriads of specific abilities, many unidentified, which are "related to one or more intermediate, more general types of intelligence" (p. 27). Gottfredson concluded that Gardner's eight intelligences and Sternberg's triarchic theory would fall in the middle level of the pyramid, indicating that all giftedness is related to basic intelligence.

There are obvious overlaps between the models addressing giftedness described above. For example, in Gardner's model, linguistic, logical-mathematical, and spatial abilities are related to some extent to those addressed by the traditional intelligence test (Lichtenberger, Volker, Kaufman, & Kaufman, 2006). Furthermore,

Sternberg's triarchic model and Gardner's linguistic and logical-mathematical abilities seem to fall within the analytical domain, and the types of intelligences in the synthetic model are very similar to the creative and artistic intelligences, such as the "musical intelligence" in Gardner's model. As for the practical domain, this encompasses Gardner's interpersonal and intrapersonal intelligences, which involve exploration of environments that are partially social or the knowledge and management of one's own strengths and weaknesses (Lichtenberger et al., 2006). Finally, Gagné's and Renzulli's models share intrapersonal and environmental intelligences.

2.4.1 Nurturing Giftedness

Whether gifted students are born gifted or are nurtured over time has been a long-held controversy. Some researchers reject the idea that genetics plays a role in giftedness or one's future success. Ericsson and Charness (1995), for example, claimed that giftedness or excellence is gained from extensive training in acquired skills and knowledge, and they rejected the idea that giftedness is a result of innate abilities. They claimed that the major characteristic that gifted people possess which separates them from others is the amount of deliberate practice and the amount of time and effort that they exert in order to achieve their success. Researchers such as Howe, Davidson, and Sloboda (1998) endorsed this view and further added that successful people do not possess any special talents when they are younger but instead work hard to become highly achieved adults.

Gifted children can be nurtured in many different ways. Usually the parents or caregivers nurture their child's giftedness by exposing their child to different cultural environments, providing lessons in their child's specialized areas, allowing the child to have easy access to books and other educational materials, and providing tutoring. By modeling self-study skills, setting high expectations for academic achievement, modeling a love for meaningful work, or direct teaching, a child can proliferate in his/her environment (Olszewski-Kubilius, 2008). Moreover, children with a high IQ tend to have parents that place major stress on achievement (Herskovits, 2000). Still, Gallagher (2008) asserted that even if a child exhibited a "favorable set of genes" but has parents who were oblivious or disinterested, and did not nurture the ability shown by their child, this did not mean that the child is not gifted or "doomed to never show his/her innate talent" (p. 3). At the same time, learning experiments done by Kandel (2006) and LeDoux (2003) recognized that intellectual abilities can grow from interactions with rich environments. Thus intelligence is to some extent modifiable; there is a direct correlation between a child's intellectual growth and the level of enrichment experienced (Clark, 2013).

On the other hand, research also shows the importance of having innate abilities. For example, Simonton (1999) portrayed giftedness as genetic traits that show up at different times within each individual according to inherited epigenetic trajectories. The same talent can surface in different people at different times.

2.4 Definitions of Giftedness

The concept of giftedness has not always been the same. Throughout history, many educators and scientists have attempted to explain giftedness. Below is a brief summary of the development of the concept of giftedness and how it evolved from a "fixed intelligence" to a "multidimensional intelligence" (Clark, 2013).

If we go back in time, one of the first pioneers of giftedness was Francis Galton. In 1869, Galton explored the inheritability of human intelligence and the differences between individuals. He also came up with the term "fixed intelligence," which means a person is born with a predetermined ability to think or process ideas and information. This process and speed of thinking will remain fixed as their inherited mental ability all throughout the individual's life. Years later, Alfred Binet developed intelligence scales, the IQ, and the concept of mental age. The IQ was designed to separate slower from faster learners. In 1921, Lewis Terman revised the Binet Intelligence Scale and created the Stanford-Binet Intelligence Scale. During the 1930s and 1940s, measuring intelligence became very popular, especially in the US army and in schools. Moreover, during this time and up until the 1970s, others such as Montessori, Wellman, Skeels, Dye, Dennis, and Hunt developed more concepts and distinctions regarding the educability of intelligence and the inconsistency of IQ and introduced interactive intelligence. In 1952, Jean Piaget developed the idea that stages and development of intelligence involved active participation from the child and endorsed the interactive view of intelligence. Four years later in 1956, at the American Psychological Association, Joy Paul Guilford introduced the Structure of Intellect model that expanded the view of giftedness and included 120 new intelligence factors, which also focused on creativity and divergent thinking. Then, during the 1960s, Vygotsky's work from the 1920s finally reached the United States where it challenged the very idea of "fixed intelligence," by indicating that early learning leads to maturation of intelligence. At the same time, other researchers such as Hunt, Bruner, Kagan, and so on created a database for interactive intelligence. During this period, researchers were moving away from the idea of fixed intelligence and were moving toward the idea that intelligence is interactive and can be matured and developed. In 1964, Bloom increased awareness of the importance of preschool learning as a vehicle for maturing intelligence in children. He also advocated the interactive intelligence theory.

More recently, in 1983, Howard Gardner introduced the theory of multiple intelligences and included linguistic, musical, logical-mathematical, spatial, bodily-kinesthetic, interpersonal and intrapersonal intelligences. IQ in itself was no longer the sole factor in identifying intelligence. A year later, Robert Sternberg created the triarchic concept of intelligence, and he included meta-processes, performance processes, and knowledge-acquisition processes with intelligence. In 1995, the concept of intelligence became multidimensional and was defined as an interaction between inherited intelligence and the environment.

In 2000, contemporary researchers such as Diamond, Kandel, LeDoux, Siegel, and other neuroscientists shifted from the behavioral definition of intelligence and began investigating how intelligence operates and develops within the brain. In 2004, Hawkins suggested a new framework of intelligence that is based on knowledge of brain function, to the point that since 2010, researchers have continued investigating the relationship between the brain and the development of intelligence.

One of the most prominent giftedness models used in this current empirical period is the Munich Model of Giftedness (MMG). MMG conceptualized giftedness as a:

> ...multifactorized ability construct within a network of noncognitive (e.g., motivation, interests, self-concept, control expectation) and social moderators which are related to the giftedness factors (predictors) and the exceptional performance areas (criterion variable)... Furthermore, the MMG represents a typological model of giftedness or talent. (Heller & Schofield, 2008, p.95)

The study done by Plomin and Price (2003) maintained that heredity factors and environmental factors are not mutually exclusive: they are not separate, and giftedness is a complex and successive set of interactions between the two. Sternberg (1996) had also concluded that intelligence is not completely environmental, nor is it unmodifiable. Yet despite the fact that lots of research has been done on other characteristics of giftedness, many teachers and researchers continue to believe that the IQ test is the ultimate tool for identifying giftedness.

2.4.2 Giftedness and Culture

Giftedness can be found in all cultures and is expressed through a variety of behaviors (Baldwin, 2005). However, the identification of giftedness is extremely complex not to mention controversial and has stimulated much debate (Al-Hroub, 2010a, 2010b, 2013, 2014; Sarouphim & Maker, 2010). Usually definitions reflect an existing cultural understanding of giftedness. These definitions can be either publicized and accepted by society or used by giftedness researchers and professionals or are based on the perceptions that are held in each society (Şahin, 2013).

Primarily, a definition of culture needs to be established. The definition that most fits our purpose is by Shade, Kelly, and Oberg (1997) which states: "culture is a social system that represents an accumulation of beliefs, attitudes, habits, values and practices that serve as a filter through which a group of people view and respond to the world in which they live" (p. 19).

According to Robert Serpell (2000), the relationship between culture and intelligence is divided into three different perspectives that he summarized under the following metaphors: culture as a language, culture as a womb, and culture as a forum. *Culture as a language* means:

> Each human culture constitutes a distinctive system of meanings for representing the mind, within which the concept of intelligence is defined. According to the *culture as a womb* metaphor, different human cultures generate different kinds of nurturing environments for the growth of a person that stimulate or mould the development of the individual's intelligence in different ways. According to the *culture as a forum* metaphor, the society and customs shared by a community gives rise to, and feeds off, debates among its members about specific matters (such as how to organize education) based on the preoc-

cupations of various participants in those debates which assign particular significances to intelligence. (p. 549)

As Serpell (2000) noted, "its range of connotations includes not only a particular set of mental functions but also the value-laden concepts of appropriateness, competence, and potential" (p. 549). An example of this will be given by comparing the meaning of intelligence between Western culture and African culture. English usage of the term intelligence can be clustered around the following characteristics: "clever, sensible, witty, observant, critical, experimental, quick-witted, cunning, wise, judicious, and scrupulous" (Serpell, 2000, p. 45). In the United States and other English-speaking industrialized societies, a person with a few of the above characteristics is considered someone who will succeed in his or her life. In contrast, some African tribes attribute intelligence using more African cultural values indicators: showing respect for elders, caring for young children, and showing attentiveness, understanding, trustworthiness, and obedience. They put more emphasis on cooperation and responsibility (Serpell, 2000). It is indeed very interesting on how different the perceptions of intelligence can be. Another example by Tobin, Wu, and Davidson (1989) states that teachers and other professionals in the United States readily acknowledge the possibility that a child who behaves antisocially at school might be intellectually gifted. Yet, a sample of teachers and parents in Japan (another highly industrialized society) reacted to such a suggestion with puzzlement. As one of them put it, "If he's so smart, how come he doesn't understand how to behave better?" (p. 550).

2.4.3 *Underrepresentation Due to Cultural Factors*

There is a major underrepresentation of diverse students in gifted programs. Ford and Harmon (2002) stated that the main reason for this underrepresentation is, as they call it, a "deficit perspective" which influences the access of gifted, culturally diverse students into gifted programs. This perspective assumes that students who are economically disadvantaged and who come from minority populations are "cognitively inferior," because they fail to meet the traditional criteria – which is scoring on the 97th percentile or above – for placement in gifted programs. As a result, lower-economic and cultural minority students are underrepresented in gifted programs. This underrepresentation is estimated to be about 30–70% relative to their percentage in the population (Gabelko & Sosniak, 2002). This cognitive-deficit hypothesis implies that most schools are using this narrow traditional definition of giftedness and intelligence (Ford & Harmon, 2002). Bernal (2002) concurs with this and adds that this definition has a major limitation because it does not take into consideration cultural factors in determining gifted cognitive abilities. Consequently, because of this traditional, widespread belief, "identification procedures in most school districts (about 90%) still rely heavily on the scores of standardized tests, a practice that limits the access of culturally diverse students to programs for the gifted and keeps the demographics of these programs mostly White" (Ford & Harmon, 2001, p. 62). This presents a big problem to gifted minority students. According to Sarouphim and Maker (2010), scholars have called for a paradigm shift in identification procedures.

This is not the only problem. There is also the issue of inadequate policies and practices that also plays a role in the underrepresentation of gifted students from minority groups. Some policies in the United States, for example, require that gifted education screening must first begin with a teacher referral, and this poses a problem because teachers (even culturally diverse teachers) under-refer students for gifted services (Colangelo & Davis, 2003). This is problematic especially if teacher referral is the only recruitment step for identification of the potentially gifted, because teacher referrals are often subjective and rely heavily on expectations and perceptions of students (Colangelo & Davis, 2003). It is even more problematic if the teachers themselves are unclear about what defines a gifted student and if there is no consensus on the definition of giftedness. To sum up, in the words of Kaufman and Sternberg (2008):

> ...conceptions of giftedness can and do change over time and place. At times in the past, a child's ability to learn classical Greek and Latin rapidly might have been viewed as an important sign of giftedness. Today, such an ability generally would be relatively less valued. Similarly, the skills that lead a child to be labeled gifted might be different in a hunting and gathering village in rural Tanzania than in urban Los Angeles. (p. 72)

2.5 Conceptions of Giftedness Around the World

According to McCann (2007), giftedness and intelligence are individual belief-based constructions, which have led to a lot of contradictions and misconceptions in gifted education. Treffinger (2009) stated that the majority of gifted theories emerged from personal and/or societal beliefs and experiences, which become validated if they undergo empirical scientific research. Even earlier researchers such as Neisser (1979) stated that giftedness and intelligence are a cultural invention taken from what people value in their own culture. Sak (2011) endorsed this and pointed out that this cultural aspect also shapes the definition, for example, whether giftedness is God-given or nurtured. Moreover, he stated that since giftedness definitions are cultural inventions, the meanings are mostly influenced by dogmas, myths, and popular beliefs. Therefore, cultural definitions are more oriented toward people's beliefs than scientific facts.

In addition, social media, mass media, and politics often publicize popular beliefs (Sak, 2011). Since technology and media have made the world smaller, popular views in one country could spread to other countries and become popular there, too (Sak, 2011). We will explore various cultural conceptions and definitions below.

2.5.1 Conceptions of Giftedness in the Middle East

According to Khaleefa (1999) and Subhi-Yamin and Maoz (2000), Arab and Middle East research into giftedness is generally dominated by the Western view of giftedness. The problem with this, as Khaleefa (1999) stated, is that adopting the Western view without attempting to adapt it to the Arab culture is "handicapping" (p. 25). He summarized that the Arabs in the Middle East must have their own view of giftedness that is specific to their own culture and needs; otherwise, the Western view will continue to influence how Arabs identify gifted students. Sarouphim (2009) also shares this view in the beginning of this book, where she states that Arabs should not follow the Western methods blindly.

Moving on to conceptions, Subhi-Yamin (2009) stated that gifted students in the Gulf and Middle East are normally identified by having the following criteria: (1) high ability (meaning high intelligence), (2) high creativity, (3) high task commitment, and (4) behavioral characteristics. However, Jordan, Bahrain, and Egypt have added a fifth criterion for identifying gifted students, i.e., having specific academic achievement (e.g., in mathematics). According to Subhi-Yamin (2009), high intellectual ability still plays a huge role in defining giftedness in the Arabian Gulf and is often just limited to this. He elaborated, "most experts in the region define a gifted child as one who acquires and processes information and solves problems at a younger age and at a faster rate than another" (p. 1485). However, Subhi-Yamin (2009) reiterated that in the Arab Islamic culture, not only are gifted students identified using Western tools, but there is no conception of giftedness that can be labeled as originally Arabic or Islamic. Conceptions of giftedness in the Arab world are heavily, if not completely, influenced by Western conceptions. We will explore three Middle Eastern countries below in order to compare how each country defines giftedness, namely, Egypt, Iran, and Palestine. Researchers from these countries have suggested the definitions in the following paragraphs, and they do not necessarily represent official definitions of giftedness in these countries. In addition, some of these definitions are merely individual initiatives, rather than nationwide conceptions.

First, we will begin with Egypt. According to Elmenoufy (2007), giftedness is defined as "a blessing from the Creator to a few pupils which enables them to excel and perform better than their peers in special academic fields" (p. 2).

In contrast with Egypt, there is no specific Iranian definition for giftedness. Like Iran, Lebanon does not have a formal definition for giftedness. Karami and Ghahremani (2016), exploring giftedness in Iran, referred to one of the most important Iranian literary works, *The Gulistan*, by Saadi, in order to explain the development of giftedness in Iranian culture. According to Karami and Ghahremani (2016), *The Gulistan* was historically used as a guidance manuscript on how to live life, for "wise and gifted" individuals. Since there is no official definition for giftedness in Iran, the stories in *The Gulistan* provided significant insight to what were historically important gifted characteristics in the Iranian culture. Iran has been offering services and programs for gifted children since 1968, but still do not have one culturally specific definition. Instead, they drew from the Western conceptions of giftedness. Even the identification procedures and selection processes are based on Western methodologies. Khaleefa (1999) cautioned against relying solely on Western concepts, as Western concepts generally clash within the context of Iranian culture. As Khaleefa (1999) stated in his study, "This practice of importing methods of studying creativity, intelligence and giftedness without rigorous conception is handicapping" (p. 25).

Within the Iranian cultural masterpiece, *The Gulistan*, there are five main words used to describe giftedness: *Aghel and Dana* (practical intelligence), *Kheradmand* (wise/wisdom), *Hakim* (sage/sagacity), *Sehab Ferasat* (insightfulness), and *Shukhdideh* (wit). The first three words describe extrinsic giftedness, meaning they are acquired through a combination of education and life experiences, while the last two words refer to giftedness acquired intrinsically. In *The Gulistan*, giftedness is referred to as being an innate quality that can be developed through education and experience.

While referencing *The Gulistan*, Karami and Ghahremani (2016) created the Iranian hierarchical wisdom model (IHW). The IHW describes the three extrinsic aspects of giftedness (*Aghel and Dana*, *Kheradmand*, and *Hakim*), practical intelligence, wise (wisdom), and sage (sagacity), respectively, in more detail. Based on *The Gulistan*, the wisdom hierarchy is pyramid shaped and is composed of *Aghel and Dana* (practical intelligence) at the bottom of the pyramid, with Hakim (sagacity) at the top of the pyramid, symbolizing its rarity. Only a few people have "sagacity," such as Ghandhi, Omar Khayyam, Nelson Mandela, and Bozorgmehr, for a few examples. Practical intelligence refers to having high intellectual abilities and high self-awareness. "Practical intelligent" people understand their own strengths and weaknesses and are able to balance their interpersonal and intrapersonal abilities. The key components of "wisdom" – the next step up the pyramid structure of giftedness – are education, experience, and age. For example, it is wise for people to know when they should speak and when they should not speak without having adequate knowledge of the subject beforehand. Wisdom is normally associated with people who have self-control, are level-headed, and are tolerant. Finally, those who possess "sagacity," which is the rarest form of giftedness, are those who have major influences on other people. As Karami and Ghahremani (2016) stated, "All sage people are scholars, but very few scholars attain sagacity" (p. 10). Problem-solving abilities are crucial to people with sagacity and are often those who are able to solve very complex problems that others are not able to solve. Most importantly, a sagacious person is someone who leads a very simple existence and is content living an honorable and graceful life.

Finally, according to Mansour (2006), Palestinians define giftedness as students possessing the following four attributes: (1) obtaining excellence (mostly academic), (2) being able to adapt easily, (3) asynchronousness which represents students who may exhibit some drawbacks in developing socially or physically but who are advanced academically, and (4) extrinsic motivation. The Palestinian conception of excellence in the first attribute, as explained by Mansour (2006), features a person encompassing a lot of knowledge, possessing meta-cognitive abilities, transferring what was learned and applying it to real-life situations, and embodying self-management techniques. Palestinian conceptions of motivation in the fourth attribute encompass curiosity, great devotion, and perfectionism.

2.5.2 Conceptions of Giftedness in Europe

This section begins with a brief commentary on giftedness in France, where it has been debated as a construct for many years. The French generally encourage talent in sporting and artistic fields yet, not until recently have they systematically addressed academic giftedness. Normally, different courses of study would be given to students who are labeled "elite." However, Vrignaud, Bonora, and Dreux (2009) explained that educational consideration for gifted development is still in the early stages. The Ministry published a report, which stated that France needs to learn more about gifted education through developing research (Lubart, 2006).

The German culture highly values high performance, individuality, uniqueness, creativity, and innovation as characteristics of gifted individuals (Ziegler & Stoeger, 2007). Giftedness in Germany refers to students having cognitive abilities that enhance their problem-solving skills in both general and specific domains, such as mathematics, natural sciences, and social abilities (Heller, 2009). Intellectual talents are normally associated with convergent thinking, and creativity is associated with multitrack or divergent thinking.

Ancient Greece was one of the first countries to develop the idea of fostering intellectual intelligence (Matsagouras & Dougali, 2009). For example, in his book *Republic*, Plato grouped society into several classes based on intelligence. In Ancient Greece, kings and philosophers were those who achieved highly in their advanced studies. According to Plato, disciplines such as geometry and astronomy were only assigned to those who were most capable and had the highest potential (Tannenbaum, 2000).

However, in modern-day Greece, the above belief has ceased to exist. Current school systems prioritize the needs of average students, thus hindering the development of gifted students to reach their full potential. The main reason for the lack of support for gifted education, currently, is due to "a suspicion of elitism and the fear that it might lead to an undemocratic education" (Matsagouras & Dougali, 2009, p. 84).

Russia's contemporary educational system is still suffering the aftereffects of the collapse of the Soviet Union as well as general global instability, both economically and socially (Jeltova & Grigorenko, 2005). In order to better understand the Russian conception of giftedness, we will give examples of different programs and services that the Russians provide to their gifted youth.

The educational system in Russia differs from the systems in France, Germany, and Greece. In Russia, according to Hobbes (1994), the educational system is a "social contract" between students, parents, educators, central government, and local communities. The social contract is understood as a "protection in exchange for giving away their power to the government" (Kondakov, 2008). To further explain this concept, Luis Jung, a Western politician and former president of the Parliamentary Assembly of the Council of Europe, proposed several goals for gifted education, which were:

> To use gifted individuals' potential for social benefits (e.g. development of scientific research, technologies, etc.), to contribute to the personal development and happiness of gifted individuals, and lastly, to obtain spectacular results. (Ushakov, 2010. p. 337)

Although parents and gifted students may seek out self-actualization and happiness, the central Russian government's main concern is to use the gifted students' potential in order to boost the economy and the power of the state (Ushakov, 2010). According to Schwartz:

> Parallels can be found in attitudes towards giftedness, intelligence, and their genetic bases. Claims such as, 'All people are gifted' or 'Individual differences in achievements are mainly due to environment or persistence' are accepted in Western cultures, yet were cultivated in Communist Russia. On the contrary, in both the West and the USSR, claims like, 'Giftedness is a rare phenomenon mainly based upon genetics' or 'Individual difference in achievements are mainly due to genetic factors' are not welcomed. Of course, these concerns reflect only public opinion. From a scientific perspective, these statements are one-sided, and as a result, often misleading. (Schwartz, 2007, p. 37)

2.5.3 Conceptions from Other Parts of the World

In this section, conceptions of giftedness will be explored in Turkey, China, New Zealand, and some African tribes.

The definition for giftedness in Turkey, according to research done by Şahin (2013), includes personal qualifications (such as intelligence, creativity, or leadership skills) or specific interests (such as in the arts, sports, or academic areas). Sak (2011) states that there are mainly two concurrent conceptions about giftedness in Turkey. In his article, he labels them as "the trendy view" and "the worker view." The "trendy view" implies that there are many intelligences or, more specifically, that there is more than one intelligence. He compares the Turkish view of giftedness with Gardner's theory of multiple intelligences. These intelligences could include football intelligence, basketball intelligence, and even sex intelligence. Sak (2011) stated that whether or not these intelligences are scientifically proven, these views are culturally prevalent everywhere – in TV programs, commercials, and conversations. The popular conception of "the worker view" is that when one starts his/her life with nothing (homeless, unsuccessful, poor, or just started working) and then achieves success, it is through hard work that they have become gifted, without genetics playing any role in their success. According to this "working view," there is no correlation between genetics and giftedness; only through hard work does one achieve giftedness, and that "giftedness" can be applied to anyone who works hard. This worker view is very similar to the research done by Ericsson and Charness (1995) and Howe et al. (1998), in the *Nurturing Giftedness* section of this chapter, earlier.

In China, giftedness and the concept of *shen-tong* (godly children) date all the way back to imperial China (Chan, 2009). There are several references made to gifted children such as *tain-cai-er-tong* (children with heavenly abilities) or *zi-you-er-ting* (children with superior genetic endowment). Such terms reflect these historical conceptions of the Chinese people regarding giftedness. According to Shi and Zha (2000), in 1978, Chinese psychologists attempted to bring in a more neutral and statistical term to refer to giftedness that did not seem to favor nature over nurture. Because of this, they came up with the term *chao-chang-er-tong* (supernormal children), which is used especially in Mainland China. However, educators and psychologists in Hong Kong and Taiwan continue to refer to gifted students as "children with superior genetic endowment." According to Chan (1998), even though China throughout its history has always identified and nurtured gifted students, systematic education for gifted students is a recent happening and is based largely on conceptions from Western cultures.

The Chinese believe in both the nature and nurture argument. They believe that giftedness is consistent with a spectrum of *cai* (abilities) and that *tian-cai* (heavenly ability) is on the top of this hierarchy. Below heavenly (that is to say, heaven-sent or heaven-given) ability comes *ren-cai* (human ability), which comes from hard work and effortful learning. Finally, the lowest end of the spectrum is the *yong-cai* (mediocre ability), which verges on lack of ability. Confucian teaching has always stemmed from the idea that all individuals should be taught according to their level of ability or *yin-cai-shi-jiao* (Chan, 2009). Confucian teaching emphasizes that nature in itself is vital to the concept of giftedness in Chinese culture and that it is the best type of giftedness. The second best are those who "learn to know or acquire the knowledge through learning" (Analects, 16:9). But the best demonstration of giftedness, according to the Chinese culture, is the interaction between both nature and nurture (Chan, 2009).

New Zealand still to date does not possess one common definition for giftedness, but the Ministry of Education published a handbook in 2000 entitled *Gifted and Talented Students: Meeting Their Needs in New Zealand Schools*. The book emphasizes the "developmentalist" view of giftedness and rejects the "fixed" view of giftedness (Tapper, 2012). Some researchers (e.g., Knudson, 2006) support this definition. Those researchers argue for the conception of "potential" giftedness, which describes a developmental approach to identifying gifted students. According to Knudson (2006), this conception of giftedness may change overtime because it is affected by environmental factors and valued by different cultures, and therefore cultural diversity should be recognized in any definition of giftedness. Bevan-Brown (2009) gave a further elaboration on this conception:

> In New Zealand, there is what is known as the Maori concept, which is a recognition of giftedness in a group context, a belief that one's talents should be used to benefit a community, that exceptional personal and moral qualities as well as outstanding skills are valued as areas of giftedness and that a strong knowledge of Maori culture and identity can be seen as an indicator of giftedness. (p. 5)

Such insights link sociocultural and domain-specific views and open a wide range of multi-categorical approaches for defining giftedness (Bevan-Brown, 2009).

We move on to central South Africa. As previously mentioned, African cultures differ from Western cultures. They believe that the individual serves the whole community. For example, the Shona, a tribal people of central South Africa, view giftedness as "a service to the community" (Mpofu, Ngara, & Gudyanga, 2007, p. 239). Moreover, they believe that giftedness could be in more than one domain. These domains include "agricultural-subsistence economies and social needs of family and clan affiliations, including spiritual supplication with the departed ancestors" (Mpofu et al., 2007, p. 240). In Kenya, Grigorenko et al. (2001) studied Kenyan conceptions of giftedness and discovered that there are four elements constituting conceptions of intelligence: (1) *rieko* (knowledge and skills), (2) *luoro* (respect), (3) *winjo* (the skills to solve real-life problems), and (4) *paro* (initiative).

2.6 Teachers' Conceptions About Giftedness

This section is a collection of several studies found in the literature regarding teachers' perceptions of giftedness. According to Freeman (2003):

> The choice of children as gifted depends neither on their high-level potential nor even their manifest excellence in any field of endeavor. Selecting for giftedness depends on what is being looked for in the first place, whether it is tested academic excellence for formal education, innovation for business, solving paper-and-pencil puzzles for an IQ club, gaining entry to a summer program for the gifted and talented or competitive athletics for one's country. Choice as gifted without testing could be affected by, for example, the interaction between the personalities of everyone concerned, what the children look and behave like, the agreed definition of giftedness, or even the percentages of ethnic representation demanded by educational authorities. Parental choice is beset by cultural stereotypes, usually meaning that two boys are chosen for every girl; a strangely stable gender proportion found all over the world, from Britain to China. (p. 2)

Interestingly, different cultures perceive giftedness in different ways. For example, Alencar, Fleith, and Arancibia (2009) found that teachers in Argentina nominated students for gifted programs based solely on high intellectual ability and academic achievement above mean scores. These teachers perceive that academic achievement and high scores are what truly define a gifted student. On the other hand, Okagaki and Sternberg (1993) found that for minority students, effort was the most important characteristic in their parents' and teachers' conception of intelligence. Nelson, McInerney, and Craven (2004) found that in countries like Papua New Guinea, teacher's recognition of giftedness included the ability to have the skills and knowledge for life in the workforce and to have skills in village-based living.

Lee (2006) also researched the perceptions of teachers in the process of identification and asked them to describe gifted children, using a qualitative research method. He studied 16 early childhood teachers. Lee's research findings revealed that the teachers understand giftedness as a series of conceptions, such as excellence, potential, rarity, behavior, innate ability, motivation, and asynchrony. In his study, Lee also found that the teachers tended to nominate more boys than girls for giftedness.

In their study, Moon and Brighton (2008) revealed that primary-grade teachers tended to hold more traditional beliefs regarding gifted children and found it hard to believe that a gifted student could come from a minority group or from a low-socioeconomic background. Specifically, their study indicated that elementary teachers continue to hold traditional conceptions of giftedness, especially with students of non-English-speaking cultural minorities. They defined and described a gifted student as having strong language skills, vast general knowledge, strong reasoning skills, and strong logical-mathematical skills, which are associated with gifted characteristics in economically advantaged students; at the same time, teachers had great difficulty conceptualizing gifted students from impoverished family backgrounds.

Teachers' beliefs, biases, attitudes, and expectations influence whether or not a student is recommended for a gifted program. A student's socioeconomic status has been proven to have a major effect on teachers' perceptions of giftedness and hence their decision-making regarding placement in gifted programs (Moon & Brighton, 2008; Rohrer, 1995). At one school level particularly, Rohrer (1995) concurred and found that the socioeconomic status of the students played an important factor in kindergarten and first-grade teachers' perceptions of giftedness. Teachers were more likely to nominate students who came from two parent houses, had educated parents, or shared some other type of higher class or high-socioeconomic-related characteristic. Unfortunately, in concurrence with Rohrer's findings, Moon and Brighton (2008) found that a quarter of the teachers in their study believed that one of the major predictors of giftedness was the student's socioeconomic status. Teachers in Brighton and Moon's study seemed to believe that gifted services were most appropriate for students who demonstrated all the traditional characteristics of giftedness, on the condition that the student *had no deficits*. Their findings also indicated that the teachers tended not to identify a gifted student if they came from minority groups or came from backgrounds different from their own. The respondents felt that a student must be able to overcome their deficits before they could be considered as gifted.

A study done by Neumeister, Adams, Pierce, Cassady, and Dixon (2007) also revealed that elementary teachers held narrow conceptions of giftedness and were not aware that culture and environmental factors may "get in the way" of the identification process of minority and economically disadvantaged students. The teachers were also "concerned" that one third of their students might be considered qualified to enter gifted programs. The basis of their concern, they agreed, was that some of these "qualified" students had a deficit in one area (e.g., poor work habits or behavioral problems). They were less likely to encourage these students to be accepted into gifted programs. In a study done by Bishofberger (2012), the findings revealed that teachers were more likely to nominate students for gifted programs based on "textbook indicators" such as the following: "can apply his/her understanding of concepts in new contexts," "is able to produce solutions when no one else can," "is able to see cause and effect relationships," and "takes the lead in small groups." These are just a few examples of textbook indicators. These indicators were preferred by teachers much more than other indicators such as teacher-pleasing characteristics, nonconformity, or incongruence. Nonetheless, teacher-pleasing characteristics were rated as the second highest dimension in perceived characteristics of gifted students. Teacher-pleasing characteristics include students who were generally compliant, knew how to please the teacher, and exhibited highly desirable classroom behavior. Other seemingly antithetical indicators consist of nonconforming behaviors, such as challenging authority, not abiding by school rules, lack of motivation, or lack of interest in learning new things. In Bishofberger's (2012) study, she found that teachers were "neutral" regarding this dimension, meaning that teachers were "neither likely nor unlikely to use 'nonconforming' characteristics as indicators of giftedness" (p. 64). Bishofberger said that this was a positive finding, because it indicates that teachers *were not set against* students who were "difficult" or "nonconforming." Teachers might select students who fought against authority and might recognize them as gifted despite their problematic behavior. However, Bishofberger revealed that teachers were still highly unlikely to select students from the last dimension, i.e., those who portrayed "incongruent" behaviors, such as having a limited vocabulary, having a limited capacity to work independently, or having "follower" qualities (Bishofberger, 2012).

2.7 Characteristics and Attributes of Gifted Learners

According to Heller and Schofield (2008), there are several behavioral indicators that characterize gifted students, which are cognitive aptitudes such as intellectual precocity, quick comprehension and high speed of learning, being quick to pick up concepts often ahead of the usual time (needed by one's age-mates), distinct curiosity, a large vocabulary for one's age, creative (original) ideas and methods to solve complex problems and individually challenging tasks or questions, eminent cognitive abilities to think convergently (as indicators of intelligence) and divergently (as indicators of creativity), sensitivity for problems, spontaneous inclination toward challenging and difficult tasks and thought problems, distinctive meta-cognitive competencies, etc. (Heller & Schofield, 2008). Another common characteristic ascribed to gifted students is heightened sensitivity, along with awareness (Mendaglio, 1995).

Children who are gifted differ not only physically but also in cognitive and language abilities, interests, learning styles, motivation, energy levels, personalities, mental health, self-concepts, habits, behaviors, and, most importantly, their educational needs (Rimm et al., 2018). Referring back to the Terman studies, his findings suggested that students who are gifted are not only more intelligent than other children are but are better adjusted psychologically, socially, and even physically. This directly opposes what Lombroso had said in 1895, a century or so back, when he claimed:

> signs of degeneration in men of genius included stuttering, short stature, general emaciation, sickly color, rickets (leading to club footedness, lameness, or a hunched back), bald-

ness, amnesia, sterility, and that awful symptom of brain degeneration – left handedness."
(As cited in Rimm et al., 2018, p. 32)

Apparently, Lombroso's declaration was widely accepted, and this made "average" people feel good about being "average." However, Terman completely challenged this myth when he claimed that people who are gifted are not only well-adjusted in the progress of their daily lives, emotionally stable, and have greater success but also show a below average incidence of suicide and mental illnesses (Sears, 1979; Terman & Oden, 1947, 1959). In 1947, Terman and Oden summarized the main characteristics of gifted children:

> For the fields of subject matter covered in our tests, the superiority of gifted over unselected children was greater in reading, language usage, arithmetical reasoning, science, literature, and the arts. In arithmetical computation, spelling and factual information about history and civics, the superiority of the gifted was somewhat less marked.... (p. 225)

They also concluded in their study that gifted children learn how to read easier and have spontaneous interests and read "more advanced" books than the average child. They also said that gifted children are better at playing games and acquire more hobbies. In addition, compared to the other children, gifted children generally score higher on emotional stability tests. As for other aspects, such as physical health, gifted children learn to talk earlier, walk around a month earlier than the average child, have greater breathing capacity, have fewer headaches, and so on. However, Terman and Oden also admit that the socioeconomic factor comes to play when talking about the health of gifted students (Terman & Oden, 1947). One must keep in mind, however, that in Terman's study, those that were identified as being gifted by their teachers were more likely to be chosen out of the "more pleasant," "well-behaved," attractive students who spoke more standard English than other students; it would appear that there was a bias, when the identification process was taking place. Rimm et al. (2018) gave the example that Terman's conclusions do not necessarily apply to those students who have great artistic talent yet are irritable, rebellious, and "undesirable."

What does it mean to be gifted in terms of observable behavior and attributes, rather than the traditional raw measurable intelligence? Intellectual characteristics will be covered first (such as precocious language and thought, logical thinking, early math, art and music, motivation, persistence, and advanced interests) and then affective characteristics (such as social skills, personal adjustment, self-concepts, independence, self-confidence, internal control, preferred styles of learning, instruction, thinking and expression, humor, and, finally, high moral thinking and empathy).

Precocious language and thought, according to VanTassel-Baska (2003), is the overriding trait of giftedness. She named precocity as the first of the three characteristics relevant to gifted curriculum planning, the other two being intensity and complexity. Similarly, Binet described gifted children as having a "higher mental age," in correlation with their chronological age. Finally, Silverman (1993a, 1993b, 2002, 2003) and many others refer to intellectual giftedness as "asynchronous" development characterized by advanced cognitive abilities. In other words, gifted children's mental or cognitive development surpasses their chronological development (or physical development). Jackson (1988, 2003) illustrates this when he points out that in some cases, gifted children are able to draw recognizable pictures or use elaborate language at age 2½, or are able to begin reading by the age of 3, and finally, are able to read fluently by the age of 4. However, Rimm and other colleagues add that not all gifted children had superb reading ability. They assert that Albert Einstein did not learn how to read until he was 8 years old, and Picasso's reading tutors quit teaching him one after the other. The most important aspect of language skills for gifted children is their comprehension skills. Gifted students are able to learn a large amount of vocabulary and are able to grasp complex, not to mention abstract, concepts that are usually learned at an older age. Finally, gifted children are able to write well at a precocious age. Although intrinsic mental readiness helps greatly with this, we should not undermine parental involvement, teacher skill, and the child's strong drive to learn, when it comes to the gifted child's writing skills (Rimm et al., 2018).

As for logical thinking, compared to the average child, the gifted students' thinking processes are both quick and more logical. They are not easily appeased with the quick response of "because" if they ask the question "why." Therefore, it is not surprising that questioning abilities, good understanding of cause-effect relationships, problem-solving, persistence, and insight are constantly mentioned as traits of gifted students in the literature (Rimm et al., 2018).

In parallel with verbal and conceptual skills are the advanced mathematical, musical, and artistic abilities. For example, a mathematically gifted preschool child may be counting by fives and tens and adding and subtracting two-digit numbers (Rimm et al., 2018). Not surprisingly, that child may have his/her own way of coming up with a mathematical solution for these problems. An example given by Rimm et al. (2018) is when a child concluded that since temperatures can go below zero, numbers below zero must logically exist. Artistically, gifted children also differ dramatically from other children. According to Winner and Martino (2000, 2003), artistically gifted children learn rapidly how to draw at a very early age, and they have superior visual memories, have great problem-solving skills, and learn virtually all by themselves. Winner and Martino (2000) also talk about musical giftedness and the fact that it may appear somewhere between the ages of 1 and 2. One could be alert to whether or not their child is gifted at this age if the child was enthralled by musical sounds. Mozart, at age 4, composed a harpsichord concerto, and at age 7, Yehudi Menuhim performed with symphonies. Rimm and his colleagues clarify that in order to be musically gifted, a child usually has an innate understanding of music structure (i.e., tonality, key, harmony, and rhythm) and the ability to hear expressive properties (such as timbre, loudness, articulation, and phrasing). They have great sensitivity with regard to the above things, not to mention a strong "musical memory," which allows the child to remember the music, play it back vocally or with an instrument, and sometimes even improvise with the music.

Another noticeable characteristic in gifted children is their continual motivation, their persistence, and their advanced interests. Rimm and his colleagues assert:

The high motivation and urge to learn found in gifted children, combined with their curiosity and their advanced comprehension and logical abilities, can lead to surprisingly advanced academic accomplishments. One group of gifted elementary students in Manitowish Waters, Wisconsin conducted an environmental impact study that led to the State Highway Department moving a section of the proposed freeway, for example, and found that persistence was related to both achievement and personal adjustment. (Rimm et al., 2018, p. 36)

Siegle and McCoach (2005) found that gifted students score higher on "intrinsic" motivation than on other measures of motivation. They reviewed several studies that showed that gifted students score higher on measures of motivation that:

Reflect intrinsic reasons for learning, including internal locus of control and measures of intrinsic motivation and autonomy. They also found that gifted students are more likely to demonstrate positive attributions for success and failure, for example, attributing success to their own ability and effort, and attributing failure to bad luck or inappropriate strategy choice. (p. 26)

Gottfried, Gottfried, and Guerin (2006) adopted a unique approach on motivation and giftedness. In their longitudinal study of intellectual and motivational giftedness, they investigated high academic motivation as a form of giftedness in itself.

We now move on to the affective characteristics of the gifted (social skills, personal adjustment, self-concepts, independence, self-confidence, internal control, preferred styles of learning, instruction, thinking and expression, humor, high moral thinking, and empathy). As Gagné's (2004) multidimensional conceptions of giftedness states, in order to achieve extraordinary things, a student must not only have intellectual excellence but should also have non-intellective (affective) elements such as intrinsic motivation and temperament.

According to Hollingworth (1942), the level of giftedness affects social skills. In her studies, she found that students with IQs ranging from 140 to 160 tended to have more friends, were well-adjusted, and were more successful in general. However, Hollingworth noted that children with IQs above 180 felt too different and had difficulty adjusting socially. Gross (2003), in concurrence with Hollingworth, showed that students with a very high IQ have poor social skills. In her study, she studied 15 Australian children with very high IQ scores (all the students scored 160, except three students who scored over 200). According to the study, their social self-esteem scores on the Coopersmith Self-Esteem Inventory (Coopersmith, 1981) were significantly below average. The students were aware that they were greatly disliked by the other students. Contrary to the above research, a recent study done by Ishak, Abidin, and Bakar (2014) revealed that gifted students do have empathetic understanding and a wide range of social skills. However, in the same study, results revealed that although gifted students were more empathetic and had positive social skills, they also showed some difficulty in creating bonds with other students. Another study done by Bakar, Ishak, and Abidin (2014) found that gifted students still scored very high in empathy, especially in the ability to interact with a diverse group of people. Gifted students also scored high in the ability to provide services and meet the needs of other students, had a high awareness of politics, and had a higher sensitivity to nature. Moreover, leadership skills were shown to have a positive correlation with empathy.

Meier, Vogl, and Preckel (2014) included self-regulatory strategies and effort as prominent characteristics that define a gifted student. Academic self-concept and self-creating goals are pivotal constructs that are being recognized more in current research (Richardson, Abraham, & Bond, 2012; von Stumm & Ackerman, 2013). Academic self-concept refers to how a student self-evaluates himself/herself in any domain (be it academic or nonacademic). Niepel, Brunner, and Preckel (2014) found that academic self-concept and achievement are reciprocal; gifted students tend to have a more positive academic self-concept compared to regular students. As for academic interest, Meier et al. (2014) reported that gifted students pay more attention in class than regular students, especially if these subjects are interesting to them.

2.8 Conclusion

The definitions of giftedness have evolved over time to encapsulate a wide range of skills and emotions. IQ test scores were the baseline for defining giftedness, before the need to include a set of interacting factors, such as motivation, humor, persistence, social skills, and logical thinking. Although the literature on giftedness has expanded, many cultures, especially in the Middle East, still nominate students based on high IQ scores. There seems to be a huge gap between the literature and what is happening on the ground. Many countries are still unsettled regarding giftedness and have been for the past hundred years. Not only are the definitions of giftedness unclear, but there are still many cases where there is underrepresentation of minority populations and students from different socioeconomic backgrounds who are not being identified because of cultural, language, and stereotype barriers. Moreover, Elhoweris, Mutua, Alsheikh, and Holloway (2005) found a strong association between the students' race, ethnicity, or socioeconomic ranking and gifted program referrals. Cultural factors are important when identifying and referring gifted students. There are various conceptions, values, and identification processes in each country. What is noticeable, however, is that recognizing giftedness around the world is generally a new phenomenon. Several countries, such as Lebanon and Iran, for example, do not have a common or federal definition. Even some developed countries such as France do not have a national definition and are new to developing gifted programs. Between Eastern and Western countries, we find that there are some major fundamental differences. If we look at countries in the Far East for example, environmental influences are the dominant factors that affect giftedness (Freeman, 2005). According to Freeman (2005), every child is believed to be born with similar potential according to its generation; however, the difference in each child's performance is the rate of development and how hard each child is working. However, some countries in the Far East, such as Taiwan, Singapore, and Hong Kong, use Western attributes for identifying gifted children, where genetic influences are believed to be the dominant factors that affect giftedness. In the West, students are generally tested on their aptitudes.

Taking a closer look at Middle Eastern conceptions, we find that most of the Arab countries focus on intellectual and academic giftedness as the main characteristics that define gifted students. Following intellectual giftedness comes leadership and creativity giftedness.

The literature is rich with projected gifted student characteristics, namely, intellectual characteristics (such as precocious language and thought, logical thinking, early math, art and music, motivation, persistence, and advanced interests) and affective characteristics (such as social skills, personal adjustment, self-concepts, independence, self-confidence, internal control, preferred styles of learning, instruction, thinking and expression, humor, high moral thinking, and empathy). Unquestionably, each individual gifted student has different characteristics, and not all gifted students are the same. Some are clearly gifted despite coexisting deficits. What are the characteristics currently that teachers look for in gifted students? Despite the profusion of possible gifted student characteristics discussed throughout current academic literature, the student who excels academically dominates all other characteristics presently used by teachers in many cases.

References

Alencar, E. M. L. S., Fleith, D. S., & Arancibia, V. (2009). Gifted education and research on giftedness in South America. In L. Shavinina (Ed.), *International handbook of giftedness* (pp. 1491–1506). New York: Springer.

Al-Hroub, A. (2009). Charting self-concept, beliefs and attitudes towards mathematics among mathematically gifted pupils with learning difficulties. *Gifted and Talented International, 24*(1), 93–106.

Al-Hroub, A. (2010a). Developing assessment profiles for mathematically gifted children with learning difficulties in England. *Journal of Education for the Gifted, 34*(1), 7–44.

Al-Hroub, A. (2010b). Programming for mathematically gifted children with learning difficulties in Jordan. *Roeper Review, 32*, 259–271.

Al-Hroub, A. (2012). Theoretical issues surrounding the concept of gifted with learning difficulties. *International Journal for Research in Education, 31*, 30–60.

Al-Hroub, A. (2013). Multidimensional model for the identification of gifted children with learning disabilities. *Gifted and Talented International, 28*, 51–69.

Al-Hroub, A. (2014). Identification of dual-exceptional learners. *Procedia-Social and Behavioral Science Journal, 116*, 63–73.

Bakar, A. Y. A., Ishak, N. M., & Abidin, M. H. Z. (2014). The relationship between domains of empathy and leadership skills among gifted and talented students. *Procedia-Social and Behavioral Sciences, 116*, 765–768.

Baldwin, A. Y. (2005). Identification concerns for gifted students of diverse populations. *Theory Into Practice, 44*(2), 105–114.

Bernal, E. M. (2002). Three ways to achieve a more equitable representation of culturally and linguistically different students in GT programs. *Roeper Review, 24*(2), 82–88.

Bevan-Brown, J. (2009). Identifying and providing for gifted and talented Maori students. *Apex, 15*(4), 6–20.

Bishofberger, S. D. (2012). *Elementary teachers' perceptions of giftedness: An examination of the relationship between teacher background and gifted identification* (Doctoral dissertation). University of Tennessee, Knoxville. Retrieved from: http://trace.tennessee.edu/utk_graddiss/1270/

Bracken, B. A., & Brown, E. F. (2006). Behavioral identification and assessment of gifted and talented students. *Journal of Psychoeducational Assessment, 24*(2), 112–122.

Callahan, C. M. (2005). Identifying gifted students from underrepresented populations. *Theory Into Practice, 44*(2), 98–104.

Chan, D. W. (1998). Development of gifted education in Hong Kong. *Gifted Education International, 13*(2), 150–158.

Chan, D. W. (2009). Lay conceptions of giftedness among the Chinese people. In T. Balchin, B. Hymer, & D. J. Matthews (Eds.), *The Routledge international companion to gifted education* (pp. 115–121). Oxford, UK: Taylor & Francis Group.

Clark, B. (2013). *Growing up gifted: Developing the potential of children at home and at school.* Upper Saddle River, NJ: Pearson Education.

Colangelo, M., & Davis, G. A. (2003). *Handbook of gifted education.* Boston: Allyn and Bacon.

Coopersmith, S. (1981). *The antecedents of self-esteem.* Palo Alto, CA: Consulting Psychologists Press.

Elhoweris, H., Mutua, K., Alsheikh, N., & Holloway, P. (2005). Effect of children's ethnicity on teachers' referral and recommendation decisions in gifted and talented programs. *Remedial and Special Education, 26*(1), 25–31.

Elmenoufy, S. G. (2007). Mathematics education for the gifted in Egypt. *Proceedings of the British Society for Research into Learning Mathematics, 27*(2), 13–18.

Ericsson, K. A., & Charness, N. (1995). Expert performance: Its structure and acquisition. *American Psychologist, 49*(2), 725–747.

Ford, D. Y., & Harmon, D. A. (2001). Equity and excellence: Providing access to gifted education for culturally diverse students. *Journal of Secondary Gifted Education, 12*(3), 141–146.

Ford, D. Y., & Harmon, D. A. (2002). Equity and excellence: Providing access to gifted education for culturally diverse students. *Journal of Secondary Gifted Education, 12*(1), 141–148.

Freeman, J. (2003). Gender differences in gifted achievement in Britain and the USA. *Gifted Child Quarterly, 47*(3), 202–211.

Freeman, J. (2005). Permission to be gifted: How conceptions of giftedness can change lives. In R. Sternberg & J. Davidson (Eds.), *Conceptions of giftedness* (pp. 80–97). Cambridge: University Press.

Gabelko, N. H., & Sosniak, L. A. (2002). 'Someone just like me': When academic engagement trumps race, class, and gender. *Phi Delta Kappan, 83*(5), 400–405.

Gagné, F. (2004). Transforming gifts into talents: The DMGT as a developmental theory. In N. Colangelo & G. Davis (Eds.), *Handbook of gifted education* (3rd ed., pp. 60–74). Boston, MA: Allyn & Bacon.

Gallagher, J. J. (2008). Psychology, psychologists, and gifted students. In S. I. Pfeiffer (Ed.), *Handbook of giftedness in children* (pp. 1–11). New York: Springer.

Gardner, H. (1983). *Frames of mind: The theory of multiple intelligences.* New York: Basic Books.

Gardner, H. (1992). Assessment in context: The alternative to standardized testing. In B. R. Gifford & M. C. O'Conner (Eds.), *Changing assessment: Alternative views of aptitude, achievement, and instruction* (pp. 77–120). Boston: Kluwer.

Gardner, H. (2011). *Frames of mind: The theory of multiple intelligences.* Boston: Harvard University Press.

Gottfredson, L. S. (2003). The science and politics of intelligence in gifted education. In N. Colangelo & G. A. Davis (Eds.), *Handbook of gifted education* (3rd ed., pp. 24–40). Boston: Allyn & Bacon.

References

Gottfried, A. W., Gottfried, A. E., & Guerin, D. W. (2006). The Fullerton longitudinal study: A long-term investigation of intellectual and motivational giftedness. *Journal for the Education of the Gifted, 29*(4), 430–450.

Grigorenko, E. L., Geissler, P. W., Prince, R., Okatcha, F., Nokes, C., Kenny, D. A., et al. (2001). The organization of Luo conceptions of intelligence: A study of implicit theories in a Kenyan village. *International Journal of Behavior Development, 25*(4), 367–378.

Gross, M. U. M. (2003). International perspectives. In N. Colangelo & G. A. Davis (Eds.), *Handbook of gifted education* (3rd ed., pp. 547–557). Boston: Allyn & Bacon.

Heller, K. (2009). Gifted education from the German perspective. In T. Balchin, B. Hymer, & D. J. Matthews (Eds.), *The Routledge international companion to gifted education* (pp. 61–67). Oxford, UK: Taylor & Francis Group.

Heller, K. A., & Schofield, N. J. (2008). Identification and nurturing the gifted from an international perspective. In S. I. Pfeiffer (Ed.), *Handbook of giftedness in children* (pp. 93–114). New York: Springer US.

Herskovits, M. (2000). Family influences on the development of high ability. *Gifted Education International, 14*(3), 237–246.

Hobbes, T. (1994). *Edwin Curley*. Indianapolis and Cambridge: Hackett Publishing Company.

Hollingworth, L. (1942). Children above 180 IQ. *The Teachers College Record, 44*(1), 56–56.

Howe, M. J., Davidson, J. W., & Sloboda, J. A. (1998). Innate talents: Reality or myth? *Behavioral and Brain Sciences, 21*(03), 399–407.

Ishak, N. M., Abidin, M. H. Z., & Bakar, A. Y. A. (2014). Dimensions of social skills and their relationship with empathy among gifted and talented students in Malaysia. *Procedia-Social and Behavioral Sciences, 116*, 750–753.

Jackson, N. E. (1988). Precocious reading ability: What does it mean? *Gifted Child Quarterly, 32*(1), 196–199.

Jackson, N. E. (2003). Young gifted children. In N. Colangelo & G. A. Davis (Eds.), *Handbook of gifted education* (3rd ed., pp. 470–482). Boston: Allyn & Bacon.

Jeltova, I., & Grigorenko, E. L. (2005). Systemic approaches to giftedness: Contributions of Russian psychology. In R. J. Sternberg & J. Davidson (Eds.), *Conceptions of giftedness* (pp. 171–186). Cambridge, UK: Cambridge University Press.

Kandel, E. R. (2006). *In search of memory: The emergence of a new science of mind*. New York: Norton.

Karami, S., & Ghahremani, M. (2016). Toward an Iranian conception of giftedness. *Gifted and Talented International, 31*, 4–18.

Kaufman, S. B., & Sternberg, R. J. (2008). Conceptions of giftedness. In S. I. Pfeiffer (Ed.), *Handbook of giftedness in children* (pp. 71–91). New York: Springer US.

Khaleefa, O. (1999). Research on creativity, intelligence and giftedness: The case of the Arab world. *Gifted and Talented International, 14*(1), 21–29.

Knudson, D. (2006). *Gifted education in New Zealand primary schools 1878–2005*. Wellington: NZCER Press.

Kondakov, A. M. (2008). *Contseptsya federalnyh gosudarstvennyh obrasovatelnyh standartov obshego obrasovanya [conception of federal state high school standards]*. Moscow: Prosveschenie. (In Russian).

LeDoux, J. (2003). *Synaptic self: How our brains become who we are*. New York: Penguin Books.

Lee Corbin, H., & Denicolo, P. (1998). Portraits of the able child: Highlights of case study research. *High Ability Studies, 9*(2), 207–218.

Lee, L. (2006). Teachers' conceptions of gifted and talented young children. *High Ability Studies, 10*(1), 183–196.

Lichtenberger, E. O., Volker, M. A., Kaufman, A. S., & Kaufman, N. L. (2006). Assessing gifted children with the Kaufman assessment battery for children—Second edition (KABC-II). *Gifted Education International, 21*(2–3), 99–126.

Lubart, T. I. (Ed.). (2006). *Enfants exceptionnels: Précocité intellectuelle, haut potentiel et talent*. Rosny-sous-Bois: Bréal.

Maker, C. J. (1996). Identification of gifted minority students: A national problem, needed changes and a promising solution. *Gifted Child Quarterly, 40*(1), 41–50.

Mansour, F. A. (2006). *Gifted education in Jenin District-Palestine: Culture, assumptions and values*. University of Cambridge: Unpublished Doctoral dissertation.

Marland, S., Jr. (1972). *Education of the gifted and talented*. Report to the Congress of the United States by the U.S. Commissioner of Education. Washington, DC: U.S. Government Printing Office.

Matsagouras, E. G., & Dougali, E. (2009). A proposal for gifted education in reluctant schools: The case of the Greek school system. In T. Balchin, B. Hymer, & D. J. Matthews (Eds.), *The Routledge international companion to gifted education* (pp. 84–96). Oxford, UK: Taylor & Francis Group.

McCann, M. (2007). Such is life… in the land down under: Conceptions of giftedness in Australia. In S. N. Philipson & M. McCann (Eds.), *Conceptions of giftedness: Sociocultural perspectives* (pp. 413–458). New Jersey: Lawrence Erlbaum Associates.

Meier, E., Vogl, K., & Preckel, F. (2014). Motivational characteristics of students in gifted classes: The pivotal role of need for cognition. *Learning and Individual Differences, 33*, 39–46.

Mendaglio, S. (1995). Sensitivity among gifted persons: A multi-faceted perspective. *Roeper Review, 17*(3), 169–172.

Moon, T. R., & Brighton, C. M. (2008). Primary teachers' conceptions of giftedness. *Journal for the Education of the Gifted, 31*(4), 447–480.

Morelock, M. J. (1992). Giftedness: The view from within. *Understanding our gifted, 4*(3), 11–15.

Mpofu, E., Ngara, C., & Gudyanga, E. (2007). Construction of giftedness among the Shona of Central-Southern Africa. In S. N. Phillipson & M. McCann (Eds.), *Conceptions of giftedness: Sociocultural perspectives* (pp. 225–252). Mahwah, NJ: Erlbaum.

Munro, J. (2002). Gifted learning disabled students. *Australian Journal of Learning Difficulties, 7*(2), 20–30.

Neisser, U. (1979). The concept of intelligence. In R. J. Sternberg & D. K. Detterman (Eds.), *Human intelligence: Perspectives on its theory and measurement* (pp. 179–189). Norwood, NJ: Albex.

Nelson, G. F., McInerney, D. M. & Craven, R. (2004). *Similarities and differences in motivation and processes of learning between Papua New Guinea and Australian school students*. Paper presented at the 3rd International Biennial SELF Research Conference on self-concept, motivation and identity, Berlin.

Neumeister, K. L., Adams, C. M., Pierce, R. L., Cassady, J. C., & Dixon, F. A. (2007). Fourth-grade teachers' perceptions of giftedness: Implications for identifying and serving diverse gifted students. *Journal for the Education of the Gifted, 30*(4), 479–499.

Niepel, C., Brunner, M., & Preckel, F. (2014). The longitudinal interplay of students' academic self-concepts and achievements within and across domains: Replicating and extending the reciprocal internal/external frame of reference model. *Journal of Educational Psychology, 106*(4), 1170–1185.

Okagaki, L., & Sternberg, R. J. (1993). Parental beliefs and children's school performance. *Child Development, 64*(1), 36–56.

Olszewski-Kubilius, P. (2008). The role of the family in talent development. In S. I. Pfeiffer (Ed.), *Handbook of giftedness in children* (pp. 53–70). New York: Springer US.

Plomin, R., & Price, T. (2003). The relationship between genetics and intelligence. In N. Colangelo & G. Davis (Eds.), *Handbook of gifted education*. Boston: Allyn & Bacon.

Renzulli, J. (1979). What makes giftedness? Re-examining a definition. *Phi Delta Kappan, 60*(2), 180–184.

Renzulli, J. S. (1986). The three-ring conception of giftedness: A developmental model for creative productivity. In R. J. Sternberg & J. Davidson (Eds.), *Conceptions of giftedness* (pp. 53–92). New York: Cambridge University Press.

Richardson, M., Abraham, C., & Bond, R. (2012). Psychological correlates of university students' academic performance: A systematic review and meta-analysis. *Psychological Bulletin, 138*, 353–387.

References

Rimm, S., Siegle, D., & Davis, G. (2018). *Education of the gifted and talented* (7th ed.). Boston, MA: Pearson.

Robinson, A., & Clinkenbeard, P. R. (2008). History of giftedness: Perspectives from the past presage modern scholarship. In S. I. Pfeiffer (Ed.), *Handbook of giftedness in children* (pp. 13–31). New York: Springer US.

Rohrer, J. C. (1995). Primary teacher conceptions of giftedness: Image, evidence, and nonevidence. *Journal for the Education of the Gifted, 18*(3), 269–283.

Sa'dī. (1964). The Gulistan, or, the rose garden of Sa'di. (E. Rehatsek, trans.) In *Ed.* London, UK: George Allen & Unwin Limited.

Şahin, F. (2013). Issues of identification of giftedness in Turkey. *Gifted and Talented International, 28*(1–2), 207–218.

Sak, U. (2011). Prevalence of misconceptions, dogmas, and popular views about giftedness and intelligence: A case from Turkey. *High Ability Studies, 22*(2), 179–197.

Sarouphim, K. M. (1999). DISCOVER: A promising alternative assessment for the identification of gifted minorities. *Gifted Child Quarterly, 43*(4), 244–251.

Sarouphim, K. M. (2009). The use of a performance assessment for identifying gifted Lebanese students: Is DISCOVER effective? *Journal for the Education of the Gifted, 33*(2), 275–295.

Sarouphim, K. M., & Maker, C. J. (2010). Ethnic and gender differences in identifying gifted students: A multi-cultural analysis. *International Education, 39*(2), 42.

Schwartz, S. H. (2007). A theory of cultural value orientations: Explication and applications. In Y. Esmer & T. Pettersson (Eds.), *Measuring and mapping cultures: 25 years of comparative value surveys* (pp. 33–78). Leiden: Brill.

Sears, P. S. (1979). The Terman studies of genius, 1922–1972. In A. H. Passow (Ed.), *The gifted and talented: Their education and development* (pp. 75–96). Chicago IL: University of Chicago Press.

Serpell, R. (2000). Intelligence and culture. In R. J. Sternberg (Ed.), *Handbook of intelligence* (pp. 549–577). New York, NY: Cambridge University Press.

Shade, B. J., Kelly, C., & Oberg, M. (1997). *Creating culturally responsive classrooms*. Washington, DC: American Psychological Association.

Shi, J., & Zha, Z. (2000). Psychological research on and education of gifted and talented children in China. In K. Heller, F. J. Monks, R. Sternberg, & R. Subotnik (Eds.), *International handbook of research and development of giftedness and talent* (2nd ed., pp. 757–764). Oxford: Pergamon Press.

Siegle, D., & McCoach, D. B. (2005). *Motivating gifted students*. Waco, TX: Prufrock Press.

Silverman, L. K. (1993a). *Counseling the gifted and talented*. Denver: Love.

Silverman, L. K. (1993b). Counseling needs and programs for the gifted. In K. A. Heller, F. J. Mönks, & A. H. Passow (Eds.), *International handbook of research and development of giftedness and talent* (pp. 631–647). New York: Pergamon.

Silverman, L. K. (2002). Asynchronous development. In M. Neihart, S. M. Reis, N. M. Robinson, & S. M. Moon (Eds.), *Social and emotional development of gifted children: What do we know?* (pp. 145–153). Washington, DC: National Association for Gifted Children.

Silverman, L. K. (2003). Gifted children with learning disabilities. In N. Colangelo & G. A. Davis (Eds.), *Handbook of gifted education* (3rd ed., pp. 533–543). Boston: Allyn & Bacon.

Simonton, D. K. (1999). Talent and its development: An emergenic and epigenetic model. *Psychological Review, 106*(3), 435.

Sternberg, R. J. (1985). *Beyond IQ: A triarchic theory of human intelligence*. Cambridge, MA: Cambridge University Press.

Sternberg, R. J. (1996). Myths, counter-myths, and truths about intelligence. *Educational Researcher, 25*(2), 11–16.

Sternberg, R. J. (2000). Identifying and developing creative giftedness. *Roeper Review, 23*(2), 60–64.

Sternberg, R. J. (2004). Culture and intelligence. *American Psychologist, 59*(5), 325–338.

Sternberg, R. J., & Davidson, J. E. (Eds.). (2005). *Conceptions of giftedness* (2nd ed.). New York: Cambridge University Press.

Subhi-Yamin, T. (2009). Gifted education in the Arabian Gulf and the Middle Eastern regions: History, current practices, new directions, and future trends. In L. V. Shavinina (Ed.), *International handbook on giftedness* (p. 1463). 1490: Springer Netherlands.
Subhi-Yamin, T., & Maoz, N. (2000). Middle East region: Efforts, politics, programs and issues. In K. A. Heller, F. J. Mönks, R. J. Sternberg, & R. F. Subotnik (Eds.), *International handbook of giftedness and talent* (2nd ed., pp. 743–756). Oxford, UK: Elsevier.
Tannenbaum, A. J. (1979). Pre-sputnik to post-Watergate concern about the gifted. In A. H. Passow (Ed.), *The gifted and the talented* (pp. 5–27). Chicago: National Society for the Study of Education.
Tannenbaum, A. J. (2000). A history of giftedness in school and society. In K. A. Heller, F. J. Monks, R. J. Sternberg, & R. F. Subotnik (Eds.), *International handbook of giftedness and talent*. Oxford: Elsevier.
Tapper, L. (2012). Conceptions of giftedness in a global, modern world: Where are we at in Aotearoa New Zealand 2012? *APEX: The New Zealand Journal of Gifted Education, 17*(1) Retrieved from www.giftedchildren.org.nz/apex.
Terman, L. M., & Oden, M. H. (1947). *The gifted child grows up: Twenty-five years' follow-up of a superior group* (Vol. 4). Stanford, CA: Stanford University Press.
Terman, L. M., & Oden, M. H. (1959). *The gifted group at mid-life: Thirty-five years' follow-up of the superior child* (Vol. 5). Stanford, CA: Stanford University Press.
Tobin, J. J., Wu, D. Y. H., & Davidson, D. H. (1989). Preschool in three cultures: Japan. In *China and the United States*. New Haven, CT: Yale University Press.
Treffinger, D. J. (2009). Demythologizing gifted education. *Gifted Child Quarterly, 53*(4), 229–232.
Ushakov, D. V. (2010). Olympics of the mind as a method to identify giftedness: Soviet and Russian experience. *Learning and Individual Differences, 20*(4), 337–344.
VanTassel-Baska, J. (2003). What matters in curriculum for gifted learners: Reflections on theory, research, and practice. In N. Colangelo & G. A Davis (Eds.), Handbook of gifted education (3rd ed., pp. 174–183). Boston: Allyn & Bacon.
von Stumm, S., & Ackerman, P. L. (2013). Investment and intellect: A review and metaanalysis. *Psychological Bulletin, 139*, 841–869.
Vrignaud, P., Bonora, D., & Dreux, A. (2009). Education practices for gifted learners in France: An overview. In T. Balchin, B. Hymer, & D. J. Matthews (Eds.), *The Routledge international companion to gifted education* (pp. 68–75). Oxford: Taylor & Francis Group.
Winner, E., & Martino, G. (2000). Giftedness in non-academic domains: The case of the virtual arts and music. In K. A. Heller, F. J. Mönks, R. J. Sternberg, & R. F. Subotnik (Eds.), *International handbook of research and development of giftedness and talent* (2nd ed., pp. 95–110). New York: Elsevier.
Winner, E., & Martino, G. (2003). Artistic giftedness. In N. Colangelo & G. A. Davis (Eds.), *Handbook of gifted education* (3rd ed., pp. 335–349). Boston: Allyn & Bacon.
Ziegler, A., & Raul, T. (2000). Myth and reality: A review of empirical studies on giftedness. *High Ability Studies, 11*(2), 113–136.
Ziegler, A., & Stoeger, H. (2007). The Germanic view of giftedness. In S. N. Phillipson & M. McCann (Eds.), *Conceptions of giftedness: Sociocultural perspectives* (pp. 65–98). Mahwah, NJ: Erlbaum.

Chapter 3
Identification of Gifted Students: History, Tools, and Procedures

Sara El Khoury and Anies Al-Hroub

Abstract This chapter sheds light on the development of intelligence testing and the various identification tools that are currently used, especially in the Middle East. Moreover, misconceptions and misdiagnosis of gifted children are explored, along with typical stereotypes, which lead to major underrepresentation of gifted students. This chapter concludes with a critical review of the different identification procedures currently being implemented.

3.1 Introduction

Bracken and Brown (2006) asserted that appropriate gifted identification is vital, especially when discussing equity in placement. Freeman (2005) stated that "Context is all in the identification of giftedness because 'gifted' is an adjective, a description, so the recognition of individuals who are seen to merit that term depends on comparisons" (p. 1). When discussing identification, one cannot but ask three important questions: What is being identified? For what purpose is the identification being attempted? Finally, what is the process by which gifted students are being identified? These questions lead to rationalizing the aim behind the importance of identifying students who are gifted and whether it is beneficial. However, even though identification is very important, in the words of Kaufman and Sternberg (2008):

> ..."giftedness" is a label—nothing more. We are frequently asked whether such-and-such or so-and-so child is gifted. The answer depends on the criteria one sets. But there is no one absolute or "correct" set of criteria. Criteria for such labeling are a matter of opinion, nothing more, and there are many disagreements as to how the label should be applied. (p. 71)

Sara El Khoury (✉)
Department of Education, American University of Beirut, Jounieh, Lebanon
e-mail: sie07@aub.edu.lb

Anies Al-Hroub
Department of Education, Chairperson, American University of Beirut, Beirut, Lebanon
e-mail: aa111@aub.edu.lb

Heller (2005) points out that it is important to identify these students, because when giftedness is not recognized (or inaccurately identified with negative labeling), conflict may arise between these students and the social environment. Identifying students who are gifted may pose some disadvantages such as labeling, bullying, and the insecurity of some parents when trying to bond with their gifted children (Heller, 2005). In the case of labeling, conflicts may arise between the child who is gifted and their sibling(s) who are not gifted, their parents, peers, and classmates. Heller (2005) also states that "labelling problems include: social isolation, development of egocentric attitudes and behaviors, endangering or disturbing personality development and self-concept through extreme achievement pressures or too much responsibility" (p. 153).

However, the importance of identification cannot be underestimated. Students who are gifted may feel the continual lack of challenge in their classes and therefore cause major behavioral problems. They may also feel isolation due to the lack of opportunities to meet and interact with other students who are gifted. This is especially true for girls who are gifted in math and the sciences but hide or hold back this gift due to gender role expectations and therefore miss the opportunity for meeting girls who are likewise gifted (Heller, 2005). Without identification, it is not possible to develop nurturance for these gifts, and they will simply go to waste. The identification of gifted students is critical for the further development of these individuals. We believe that nurturing these gifts will bring benefit to society as a whole.

3.2 Brief History of Intelligence Testing

During the nineteenth and early twentieth centuries, the contributions of Francis Galton, Alfred Binet, Lewis Terman, and Leta Hollingworth added much to the field of gifted education. Francis Galton (1822–1911) was a young cousin of Charles Darwin. He was one of the first people to do significant research in intelligence testing. He believed that intelligence sprang from the keenness of one's senses, namely, vision, hearing, smell, touch, and reaction time (Galton, 1869). He argued that intelligence (sensory ability) is due to natural selection and heredity. In his book *Hereditary Genius* (Galton, 1869), he concluded that intelligent people generally seem to come from generations of distinguished families and that it increased the person's chance of becoming distinguished.

French Psychologist Albert Binet contributed a great deal as well. In the 1890s, he was responsible for the foundations of modern intelligence tests (Rimm, Siegle, & Davis, 2018). He came up with the notion of "mental age," which is the concept that children develop or grow in intelligence and that any child is either at the appropriate stage for his/her age or is advanced or is behind. He also stated that children who learn more do so because of greater intelligence. At first, in an attempt to distinguish between regular and gifted children, he tried to compare hand-squeezing strength, hand speed in moving them 50 cm, how much pressure could be exerted on the forehead before causing pain, differences in hand-held weights, the reaction time to sounds, or the naming/distinguishing of colors (Rimm et al., 2018). He found that there was no significant difference in these measurements between regular and gifted children. However, when he measured the ability of paying attention, memory, judgment, reasoning, and comprehension, he was finally able to obtain results that are more accurate. These tests could distinguish the gifted from the nongifted (Binet & Simon, 1905a, 1905b).

Lewis Terman, a Stanford psychologist referred to as "the father of the gifted education movement," made two very important contributions to the field of gifted education. The first came when he supervised the modification and Americanization of the Binet-Simon tests producing in 1916 the *Stanford-Binet Intelligence Scale* (Rimm et al., 2018). His second prominent contribution was his longitudinal study of 1528 gifted children that was published in the *Genetic Studies of Genius* series. Terman and his colleagues initially identified 1000 children with IQ scores above 135 (the upper 1%) using the Stanford-Binet. Later in 1928, he added 528 more children. His research involved parents, teachers, medical records, and anthropometric measurements. When he died in 1956, several researchers (Rimm et al., 2018) continued his work. The aim of Terman's research was twofold "first of all, to find what traits characterize children of high IQ, and secondly, to follow them for as many years as possible to see what kind of adults they might become" (Terman, 1954, as cited in Robinson & Clinkenbeard, 2008, p. 223). His main conclusions after conducting this long study were that highly gifted children (scoring an IQ of 140 or above) were healthier, were more adjusted, and achieved higher grades in school than other children. He also concluded that, contrary to generally stated historical beliefs, gifted students were *not* prone to mental illnesses.

Leta Hollingworth, working in the 1930s and known as the "Nurturant Mother," invented strategies that identify, teach, and counsel gifted children (Klein, 2000). Hollingworth contributed a great deal to the field of gifted education. She believed that the top 1% of the child population (IQ 130–180) should be considered gifted and that gifted children become gifted adults (Rimm et al., 2018). She believed that early identification is crucial in order to provide optimum educational experiences for the child. She also believed that schools should use multiple identification criteria when assessing a child for giftedness. Her identification procedure included IQ tests, interviews with the child and the parents, nominations from the teacher and the principal, and finally a review of each child's social and emotional maturity (Rimm et al., 2018). Interestingly, Hollingworth assumed that students with an IQ of 140 waste around half their time in school and students whose IQ level is 170 waste all their time in school (Rimm et al., 2018). Her main belief was that children who had extremely high IQ scores were more likely to have difficulty in socially adjusting to their surroundings. She stated, "To have the intelligence of an adult and the emotions of a child combined in a childish body is to encounter certain difficulties" (Hollingworth, 1931, p. 15).

Witty (1930) produced a study similar to that of Terman's. His study included a sample of 41 children who had IQs of 140 or above (he later added an additional 50 children), where he conducted a longitudinal study of more than 4 years. He collected data mainly from the schools, namely, achievement data from teachers' records of the students. Witty was also interested in collecting moral and social indicators given by parents. He believed in "domain-specific talents" (Witty, 1930, p. 24) and that these talents distinguish gifted students from their peers. The conclusions that were drawn from his study were very similar to Terman's study. However, Witty believed that giftedness does not rely solely on nature or nurture but somewhere in between. He refuted all arguments that giftedness is purely endowed by nature or that giftedness is purely sculpted by nurture. Witty concluded that giftedness includes drive and opportunity, in addition to ability (Lehman & Witty, 1927).

In 1934, Jenkins also contributed majorly to the field of gifted education. Together with his mentor Witty, they conducted a study on 26 African-American students from grades 3 to 8, in seven public schools (Witty & Jenkins, 1934). Their screening methods were very similar to those of Terman; however, the schools were very segregated at the time of their study (1930s) which is why the participants were exclusively African-American. Witty and Jenkins asked the teachers to nominate three of their best students, and later, these nominees were administered the McCall Multi-Mental Scale. Those students who scored 120 or more on this scale were given the Stanford-Binet IQ test, and the students who scored an IQ of 140 or above were chosen for the study. One of their major findings involved a 9-year-old African-American girl who scored an IQ of 200. This was extremely important, because the results proved that there existed "Negro" gifted students, despite being constantly faced with racism. They later published a case study on the girl and named the study, "The Case of 'B'—A Gifted Negro Girl" (Witty & Jenkins, 1935). That Witty and Jenkins' results contained an African-American girl was remarkable, set against Terman and Hollingworth, whose findings included only White gifted pupils. Jenkins conducted an additional study and found over 103 gifted African-American students with an IQ of 120 or above, thus proving that giftedness was not contained only within the White community. Jenkins discovered in a study he made in 1936 a larger sample of gifted *girls* than boys; 72 girls were reported to be gifted compared to only 31 boys (Jenkins, 1936). Terman's contemporaneous study had found more gifted boys than girls, and in Witty's sample, there were equal numbers of gifted girls and boys.

Finally, there came the launching of the Russian satellite Sputnik in 1957. Curiously, this was remarkable and important to our subject. "To many [American people], the launch of Sputnik was a glaring technological defeat – Russia's scientific minds had outperformed ours" (Tannenbaum, 1979). The effect of this extraordinary event led to reporters criticizing American education, specifically, in ignoring its gifted population. Tannenbaum (1979) summarizes the events that happened post-Sputnik: "Gifted students were identified. Acceleration and ability groupings were installed. Academic course work was telescoped (condensed). College courses were offered in high school. Foreign languages were taught to elementary school children and so on". Tannebaum refers to these events as a "total talent mobilization." According to Tannebaum, the awareness and concern for educating gifted children were further renewed in the mid-1970s.

3.3 Identification Tools and Procedures

As for the identification procedure itself, gifted students cannot always be identified easily (Heller, 2005). Reasons for this include prejudices, false assumptions, observational errors, lack of knowledge, and misguided information. There are other reasons for misidentifying gifted students. Some gifted students have major behavioral problems, so are often overlooked. Many gifted students are also underachievers (Ziegler & Heller, 2003); other students fail to be noticed if they are from economically disadvantaged groups or from minority groups, because they may underperform compared to the dominant group. (Heller, 2005).

For the earlier researchers such as Terman and Hollingworth, giftedness was based entirely on raw intellectual power, or IQ level, so that identification was based solely on IQ tests/scores (Bracken & Brown, 2006). It would only be after setting the minimal IQ standards for identification that researchers later would begin to investigate the other characteristics of giftedness (Bracken & Brown, 2006). Tests that have been used to measure general intellectual ability are either in the form of individually administered tests or group tests.

Individually administered tests of intellectual ability are more accurate than group tests in identifying gifted students (Assouline, 2003). Examples of individually administered tests include the Wechsler Intelligence Scale for Children, 4th Revision (WISC-IV) (Wechsler, 2003), and the Stanford-Binet Intelligence Scale (Roid, 2003). The results of the WISC-IV provide information for various areas of mental functioning and produce a full-scale IQ score (Karnes & Stephens, 2009). The Stanford-Binet Intelligence Scale produces a general measure of intelligence, rather than scores for separate abilities (Karnes & Stephens, 2009).

Though individually administered tests produce more reliable results, group tests have several advantages, namely, that they are generally inexpensive, are efficient to administer, and require minimal professional input (Karnes & Stephens, 2009). Examples of group tests include the Otis-Lennon School Abilities Test (OLSAT) (Otis & Lennon, 1995), the Cognitive Abilities Test (CogAT) (Lohman & Hagen, 2001), and the Kaufman Assessment Battery for Children, Second Edition (KABC-II) (Kaufman & Kaufman, 2004a). According to Karnes and Stephens (2009), group tests pose several disadvantages such as assessing only limited cognitive skills (reading, mathematics, language, spelling, verbal and nonverbal problem-solving abilities) while neglecting assessing other important abilities such as the thinking process that the student went through to answer the questions.

Achievement tests are also widely used as a means of identifying gifted students. The Kaufman Test of Educational Achievement, Second Edition (KTEA-II) (Kaufman & Kaufman, 2004b), is an example of an achievement test. This test is used to assess how well a student has learned a subject matter and indicates the student's overall level of reading, mathematics, and writing skill.

As the field of gifted education evolved, elitism leads to limited access to programs and resources which were only provided to the students who were part of the "intellectual club"; the criteria for admittance to this club were their Stanford-Binet or Wechsler scale scores. Because of this acknowledged elitism and due to the social pressure advocating the inclusion of more students into these gifted programs, the field began to consider different methods of identifying gifted students and alternatives to purely relying on IQ scores (Bracken & Brown, 2006). Thus identification programs began taking a more multidimensional approach not solely based on IQ scores (Al-Hroub, 2013; Pfeiffer & Jarosewich, 2003), including tools such as checklists, rating scales, and tests which assess motivation and creativity, in addition to the intellectual characteristics. Final decisions were usually based on a combination of checklists, rating scales, school report cards, and teacher/parent/peer nominations. Teachers started using teacher-completed rating scales. One of the earliest of these was the Scales for Rating the Behavioral Characteristics of Superior Students (SRBCSS) (Renzulli et al., 1976, 2002).

The SRBCSS and similar scales are worth mentioning because they have added a third party element in the process of identification. The belief was, and is, that teachers, with their experience and expertise, could add greatly to the identification process (Bracken & Brown, 2006). Teacher and parent rating scales continue to become more apparent and useful in identifying gifted students. More and more scales have been developed, and the number of behavior specifications presently used for identifying gifted students has increased to more than 30 (Jarosewich, Pfeiffer, & Morris, 2002). Jarosewich et al. (2002), for example, identified 31 scales that they collected from the literature and narrowed them down to three dominant concerns. These scales are more gifted specific but are also broader in behavior assessment and take into account more recent conceptions of giftedness (Bracken & Brown, 2006). Professionals working with gifted students in more recent times believe that gifted students exhibit more affective (social/emotional) and conative (motivational) characteristics than just a high IQ (Moon, 2003). Research findings have shown that gifted students are better adjusted than average students (Neihart, Reis, Robinson, & Moon, 2002). For example, in her book, *Growing up Gifted*, Clark (2013) supplied an overview of the screening process and possible tools to help identify gifted students. She mentions the following abilities: intellectual ability, high academic achievement, specific academic ability, creative ability, leadership ability, and ability in the visual and performing arts.

What sprang from this is the Gifted Rating Scales (GRS) (Pfeiffer & Jarosewich, 2003), and this more contemporary instrument added even more scales and a comprehensive list of behavioral indicators that coincide with recent definitions of giftedness. However, the problem with using these informal behavioral checklists, according to Moon (2007), is that these lists often mix affective, cognitive, and conative items on the same scale; for example, such heterogeneous items might be "has lots of initiative," "is an independent worker," or "has a long attention span." Quite often, these checklists are not sensitive to cultural differences.

Creativity tests were also established to move away from identifying students based only on IQ scores. The advantage of creativity tests is that they assess both cognitive abilities (such as thinking divergently, making associations, constructing and combining categories) and non-cognitive aspects of creativity (such as motivation, flexibility, and independence). The Torrance Test of Creative Thinking

(Torrance, 1970) is one such test, used to measure fluency, originality, and elaboration for creativity.

Other tools include the Scholastic Aptitude Test (SAT) which was created as a tool for talent search programs, primarily for seventh grade students (Lupkowski-Shoplik, Benbow, Assouline, & Brody, 2003). The Scholastic Aptitude Test has been renamed several times to Scholastic Assessment Test, then the SAT I: Reasoning Test, then the SAT Reasoning Test, and finally to the SAT (Coyle, Snyder, Pillow, & Kochunov, 2011). The SAT, along with other programs such as Explore and PLUS, is also used as acceptance tools for talent search programs (Olszewski-Kubilius, 2004). Other recent identification procedures include the DISCOVER model, created by Maker (2005), which evaluates problem-solving and creative abilities.

Another more recent instrument is the Clinical Assessment of Behavior (CAB) (Bracken & Keith, 2004). This instrument is a comprehensive teacher and parent behavior rating scale for children ages 2–18 years and is used to assess a diverse collection of behaviors consistent with psychosocial maladjustment and behavioral disorders, as well as adaptive behaviors. According to the authors of the CAB:

> It may have promise as an instrument for widespread identification of gifted students through objective teacher evaluations. The CAB has the benefit of being easy to administer, brief, and computer scored and interpreted; and it has excellent psychometric properties for students aged 2 through 18 years. Although the CAB has promise as a behavioral screener, additional validation work needs to be conducted to evaluate its utility as a tool in the identification of gifted and talented students. (p. 120)

Kaplan, Rodriguez, and Siegel (2000) suggested another screening option, where curricular activities could be used to assess the students' abilities, rather than discrete tools or instruments. Curricular activities could be designed in a way that gives students many opportunities to show their potential by interacting with the materials. Kaplan et al. asserted that this type of screening process could assist in identifying culturally diverse students (Clark, 2013). The tasks included in the curricular activities involve verbal abilities, where students are encouraged to express themselves via open-ended questions, prediction of action pictures, problem-solving strategies, and further methods of encouragement to express themselves creatively.

Complementing the tools and methods of identification described above, a new movement of dynamic assessment is taking place. Dynamic assessment is a complementary approach, geared to discover the potential of gifted students. It is not a stand-alone method, but rather can be used along with other psychometric test results, especially when using a multidisciplinary assessment approach. Dynamic assessment is based on the belief that a child's cognitive development can be assessed more accurately by working together with the student (so-called scaffolding), rather than assessing the student's unassisted performance (Al-Hroub, 2013). The concept of dynamic assessment was inspired by Vygotsky's work on the zone of proximal development (ZPD). The theory behind ZPD is that children will learn faster when scaffolding and adult guidance are present. The dynamic theory of giftedness (DTG) is also based on Vygotsky's developmental concept of "plus and minus giftedness" (Vygotsky, 1983). This approach is also beneficial for identifying disadvantaged, disabled, or underserved gifted children (Al-Hroub, 2013).

This is because dynamic assessment provides domain-specific diagnosis of children with learning difficulties (Al-Hroub, 2013). According to Bolig and Day (1993), there are numerous advantages of using dynamic assessment: (1) it can detect differences in learning ability among students with identical intelligence test scores; (2) it provides information that helps determine what and how to teach to individual students; (3) it was developed to overcome the shortcomings of traditional tests particularly with regard to disadvantaged students; (4) its focus is on learning ability more than knowledge; (5) it provides information on how students attempt to solve tasks by examining students' errors for signs of mistaken beliefs, gaps in knowledge, selection of incorrect strategies, and cognitive deficiencies (Cited in Al-Hroub, 2013).

Other types of tools include different types of nominations, specifically from teachers, parents, and peers. Teacher nomination evolved as an integral part of the process in identifying gifted children. McBee (2006) refers to teacher nomination as the "gatekeeper" in the first steps of the identification path. In some cases, teacher nomination serves as the sole means of identifying the gifted children. In other situations, teacher nominations are just one method of many in a sequence used to identify gifted children (Bain & Bell, 2004; Wu & Elliott, 2008). Schroth and Helfer (2008) conducted a study on school personnel's beliefs about identifying gifted students, and they found that teacher nominations were believed to be the second most effective method of identification – following performance assessments – but ranked ahead of standardized tests. Not surprisingly, however, they also found that the teacher-participants in their study ranked teacher nominations as the most effective and efficient means of identifying gifted students in the classroom. Many researchers, for example, believe that the number of African-American males that participate in gifted programs is there because the teachers who act as "gatekeepers" are the ones who recognize and promote these students entering the gifted programs (Elhoweris, Mutua, Alsheikh, & Holloway, 2005; Ford, Grantham, & Whiting, 2008; Speirs et al., 2007). In a study done in Jordan by Al-Hroub and Whitebread (2008), the findings revealed the extent to which teachers are accurate in nominating "twice-exceptional" children at the elementary school level. Their analysis showed that 57.6% of their nominations were accurate. It follows that teacher nomination is an essential initial element in the identification protocol for twice-exceptional children.

Parent nominations consist of forms, questionnaires, rating scales, or checklists that are used to provide schools with necessary information regarding their child's characteristics, skills, and behavior. Peer nominations are becoming helpful, especially when attached with other sources. Peer nominations could be in the form of checklists or questionnaires. With both parent and peer nominations, caution should be taken; as parents and peers might be subjective. It is best to have these nominations as supplements to other sources before making a final decision regarding a student's placement (Karnes & Stephens, 2009).

Recent researchers have suggested using a more flexible and multidimensional approach to identifying gifted students (e.g., Al-Hroub, 2010; Fetzer, 2000; Renzulli,

1990). This approach uses individually administered tests of intelligence, academic achievement, creativity tests, and dynamic assessments. Creativity tests are necessary as they measure abilities that cannot be found solely through cognitive ability measures (Thompson, 2001). Renzulli (1990) proposed a multi-faceted identification system structured on his three-ring model, which he transformed into an identification system. Its aim was to identify all the gifted characteristics students have, by incorporating both objective and subjective procedures. By using Renzulli's identification system, gifted students could be accurately identified regardless of their achievements in school, whether or not they were motivated, or if they exhibit bad behavior. Renzulli proposed a six-step system, as follows: *(Step 1)* test score nominations, *(Step 2)* teacher nominations, *(Step 3)* alternative pathways, *(Step 4)* special nominations, *(Step 5)* notification and orientation of parents, and *(Step 6)* action information nominations.

Step 1: it entails gathering students' scores on any type of intelligence tests. Students who score at or above the 92nd percentile would be nominated. In this step, students who score high on either or both verbal and nonverbal ability tests are entered in the "talent pool." This means that excellent students who are underachievers can be selected.

Step 2: it entails gathering information from teachers who are able to detect abilities and characteristics not measured by standard intelligence tests, such as creativity, interest, talents, and task commitment. Teacher nominations will be given equal value to the scores on the intelligence tests.

Step 3: it takes into account peer and parent nominations, creativity, and self-nominations. There is usually a screening committee in this step that interviews the selected students and administers other assessments as well.

Step 4: a list of students who have passed all of Steps 1–3 is given to all the teachers in the same school district. This gives teachers a "second chance" to consider students who might not have been chosen the first time due to bias or any other reason. This step also requires a screening committee who will interview the students nominated by the teachers during this second round.

Step 5: it requires the school to inform parents that their child has been nominated and placed in the "talent pool." Once parents have been notified and informed of the identification procedures that have taken place, an orientation session for the parents is held explaining the gifted program, and a separate one is held for the selected gifted students.

Step 6: the final step, is called "the second safety valve" (Renzulli, 1990) (the first one being Step 4) and involves "action information" which, as explained by Renzulli, is the "dynamic interactions that occur when a student becomes extremely interested in or excited about a particular topic, area of study, idea, or event" (p. 16). A nomination that occurs in Step 6 is based on a careful review in order to realize if advanced services for a particular student are necessary. In this way, it is ensured that all the students are noticed (Renzulli, 1990).

Al-Hroub (2013, 2014) also proposes a multidimensional model for identifying gifted students. In his study, he proposes a model for particularly identifying gifted students who have learning disabilities. Similar to Renzulli, Al-Hroub suggests using psychometric test results, in combination with dynamic and informal assessments, historical data, and task analysis, while also gathering information from parents, teachers, and students. This proposed model includes teacher and parent nominations and the use of school records, documentary evidence, behavioral observation, individually administered tests, perceptual skills and literacy tests, and dynamic assessment (Al-Hroub, 2010, 2013, 2014).

3.4 Identifying Students in the Middle East

As already mentioned in Chapter 2, gifted students in the Gulf and Middle East are normally identified as having the following criteria: (1) high ability (meaning high intelligence), (2) high creativity, (3) high task commitment, and (4) behavioral characteristics, with high intellectual ability being one of the main characteristics that define a gifted student (Subhi-Yamin, 2009). Based on this definition, the current identification tools that are being administered are standardized intelligence tests (*thikaá*), creativity tests (*ibdaá*), achievement tests that measure abilities (*tahseel*), rating scales such as the SRBCSS, and attitude surveys, usually toward gifted education (*itijahát*). Task commitment (*iltizam wa mothabra*) is measured through achievement tests, rating scales, and the judgment (*hukum*) usually of teachers and parents (Subhi-Yamin, 2009).

It is important to mention that according to Subhi-Yamin (1992), Arabic countries have multiple-criteria identification procedures. This is based on the following principles: (1) gifted students must be identified as early as possible in their educational careers; (2) the purpose of identifying students is *to recognize gifted students' needs*, not to label them or judge them; (3) identifying students is expected to be achieved through a mixture of formal and informal testing obtained from different sources and from different settings; and (4) all identification tools and procedures should be legitimate and in concurrence with the program that is using these instruments. The purpose of having multiple-criteria identification processes is in order to realize which student in the classroom is in need of special provisions, mainly as supplemental or alternative instruction, and to diagnose their abilities (Subhi-Yamin, 1992).

3.5 Underrepresentation of Gifted Children from Minority Groups

Gifted students from minority groups are difficult to identify for various reasons (Heller & Schofield, 2008). Some of these reasons include perceptual distortion, which occurs when teachers or caregivers lack the appropriate knowledge about how giftedness "should appear" and may have prior assumptions or prejudices toward identifying gifted students. Another problem is identifying "high-risk groups"; for example, teachers may overlook gifted students with behavior problems, gifted students with special needs, gifted girls (especially in mathematics and the sciences), and gifted underachievers (gifted students who have low performance in school) (Ziegler & Stoeger, 2003). Some gifted students may have unfavorable family and school settings (e.g., parents who may believe that giftedness only manifests itself in math, or a one-parent family, or parents who do not wish to differentiate one sibling over the others or who feel that they cannot afford to, etc.). Many more problems exist in addition to all the above. There is a major problem of underrepresentation of students from minority groups.

The underrepresentation of gifted students from minority groups continues to be a widespread problem in the field of gifted education (Ford et al., 2008; Grantham, 2003; Yoon & Gentry, 2009). The Education Trust (2003) did a sampling of education reports for 30 states in the United States and found that African-American students were underrepresented in gifted programs in 22 states, Latino students were underrepresented in 16 states, and finally, Native Americans were underrepresented in 3 states (Education Trust, 2003). More recent data on this says that, for example, even though African-American students constituted 7.60% and Latino students 48.15% of school enrolment in California during the 2006–2007 term (California Department of Education, 2009a), African-American children constituted only 4.18% of those in gifted programs and only 28.27% of students enrolled in gifted programs were Latino (California Department of Education, 2009b). Comparatively, Caucasian students constituted 29.41% and Asian students 8.12%, respectively, of the state's total school enrolment; however, Caucasian students filled 43.30% and Asian students 17.49% of the gifted program enrolment. Not surprisingly, ethnic minorities are not the only groups who are underrepresented in gifted education (Carman, 2011). Other groups who are underrepresented include students with physical or learning disabilities, English Language learners, and students living in poverty (Burney & Beilke, 2008; Cotabish, Robinson, Anthony, Bryant, & Calder-Isgrig, 2007; Lockwood, 2007).

A study was done to investigate the perceptions of fourth grade teachers regarding giftedness and identification procedures for minority gifted students, by Speirs et al. (2007). Twenty-seven teachers were surveyed. The results showed that these teachers held narrow conceptions of giftedness and were not aware that culture and environmental factors may unfavorably influence the identification process of minority and economically disadvantaged students. The teachers were also "concerned" that about one third of their students were being considered qualified to enter gifted programs. The consensus of this concern was that many of the students being identified as gifted retained a deficit in some area, such as poor work habits or behavior problems. The teachers were less likely to encourage these students from entering gifted programs (Speirs et al., 2007).

As mentioned earlier in the chapter describing conceptions, but critical to this discussion of difficulties in identifying minority gifted students, the following studies bear reference again especially given the gatekeeper role still so often attributed to teachers in the identification process. Elhoweris et al. (2005) found that teachers making referrals for hypothetical students in their study were less likely to nominate an African-American student than an identical student who was not considered African-American. Also as previously discussed, a student's socioeconomic status has been proven to have a major effect on teachers' perceptions of giftedness and hence upon their decision-making regarding placement in gifted programs (Moon & Brighton, 2008; Rohrer, 1995). Rohrer (1995) found that the socioeconomic status of the students played an important factor in kindergarten and first-grade teachers' perceptions of giftedness and that teachers were more likely to nominate students who came from two-parent houses, had educated parents, or shared some other types of higher-class or high-socioeconomic-related characteristic. Unfortunately, in concurrence with Rohrer's findings, Moon and Brighton (2008) found that a quarter of the teachers in their study believed that one of the major predictors of giftedness *is* the student's socioeconomic status. In agreement with Speirs et al. (2007) mentioned above, teachers in Brighton and Moon's study seemed to believe that gifted services are most appropriate for students who can demonstrate all the aforementioned characteristics of giftedness, on the condition that the student also *has no deficits*. The respondents suggested that the student must be able to have overcome any of these deficits before they *qualified to be considered* gifted. Moon and Brighton also found that teachers were not able to identify a gifted student if they came from minority groups or different background than their own.

While one of the main explanations for the problem of underrepresentation is the issue of teacher nominations, there are many explanations that include stereotyping (Carman, 2011), racist predispositions, and socioeconomic biases (Elhoweris et al., 2005; Grantham, 2002; Hernández-Torrano & Tursunbayeva, 2015; Hyland, 2005; Moon & Brighton, 2008; Tyler, Boykin, & Walton, 2006). Because teachers interact with and observe students more frequently in a variety of situations, they are in an advantageous position to serve a central role in identifying students who are gifted (Bracken & Brown, 2006). However, are teachers qualified to make judgments about their students' behavior? Rohrer (1995) was concerned about teacher's preconceived notions of giftedness. Rohrer noticed that on most behavior rating scales, teacher may be improperly influenced by the scale headings, item organization, and arrangement. Many times, teachers may "falsely rate the student good" or "falsely rate the student bad" depending on how they personally feel about that particular student. In spite of this, Rohrer found that many times, teachers are able to accurately recognize potentially gifted students, even if the student does not fit the criteria of the stereotypical gifted student.

3.5.1 Misconceptions and Misdiagnosis

There is a major underrepresentation of gifted students in schools. Ford and Harmon (2002) stated that the main reason for this underrepresentation is, as he calls it, a "cognitive deficit perspective" which influences the access of gifted, culturally diverse students into gifted programs. This perspective assumes that students, who are economically disadvantaged or who come from minority populations, are "cognitively inferior," because they fail to meet the traditional criteria for placement in gifted programs (i.e., scoring on the 97th percentile or above), and as a result, these students are underrepresented in gifted programs. This underrepresentation is estimated to be about 30–70% relative to their percentage in the population (Gabelko & Sosniak, 2002). If so, this implies that most schools are using this narrow and limiting cognitive deficit hypothesis definition of giftedness and intelligence (Ford et al., 2008). Bernal (2002) concurs with this and adds that this definition has major limitations because it does not take into consideration differing cultural factors in determining gifted cognitive abilities. Because of this continuing widespread belief, "identification procedures in most school districts (about 90%) still heavily rely on the scores of standardized tests, a practice that limits the access of culturally diverse students to programs for the gifted and keeps the demographics of these programs mostly White" (Ford & Harmon, 2001, p. 62). This presents a big problem for gifted minority students. According to Sarouphim and Maker (2010), scholars have called for a paradigm shift in identification procedures.

This is not the only problem. There is also the issue of inadequate policies and practices that also plays a role in the underrepresentation of gifted students from minority groups. Some policies in the United States, for example, require that gifted education screening must first begin with a teacher referral, and this poses a problem because teachers (even culturally diverse teachers) under-refer minority students for gifted services (Colangelo & Davis, 2003). This is problematic especially if teacher referral is the only recruitment step, because teacher referrals are often subjective and rely heavily on individual expectations and teachers' perceptions of students (Colangelo & Davis, 2003). It is even more problematic if the teachers themselves are unclear about what defines a gifted student and if there is no general consensus surrounding the definition of giftedness.

3.5.2 Racist Predispositions and Socioeconomic Biases

Interestingly, not all teachers value programs for the gifted (McCoach & Siegle, 2007), and it is plausible that these teachers are predisposed to not recommend students of any nationality, race, ethnicity, or gender to participate in gifted programs. Surprisingly, findings revealed that some teachers who, while supporting gifted programs, still do not recognize gifted characteristics in African-American children (Elhoweris et al., 2005; Tyler et al., 2006). The inability of those teachers to recognize gifted characteristics in Black children is related to discrimination and socioeconomic biases.

As for racist predispositions, studies in the United States found that some teachers were more likely to refer White students to gifted programs than Black or Hispanic students (Elhoweris et al., 2005). In a study done by Elhoweris et al. (2005), 207 elementary school teachers were asked to make referrals of hypothetical students to gifted programs, based on vignettes that did or did not include the student's ethnicity. The researchers found a strong association between the students' race or ethnicity and gifted program referrals. They concluded that "stereotypical notions about African-American student capabilities may serve to bar some of these students from participating in gifted and talented programs" (p. 29). Tyler et al. (2006) have done similar studies, and they came up with the same conclusion. Hyland (2005), however, concluded that teachers usually mean well and are often unaware of their racist biases.

As for purely socioeconomic biases, studies reveal that some teachers consider students who come from low-income and minority backgrounds to be "less intelligent" than other students (Moon & Brighton, 2008). They found that 35% of the teachers who participated in their study disagreed with the statement that "the potential for academic giftedness is present in all socioeconomic groups in our society" (p. 461). This relates to an earlier study done by Minner (1990), which concluded that "teachers were less inclined to refer a student from a poor or middle class background for participation in a gifted program" (p. 39).

3.5.3 Stereotyping

Stereotyping is defined as "the unconscious or conscious application of (accurate or inaccurate) knowledge of a group in judging a member of that group" (Banaji & Greenwald, 1994, p. 58). Stereotypes often center on certain behaviors, expected interests, physical attributes, activity preferences, and social functioning (Biernat & Thompson, 2002). Other aspects of stereotyping include gender, age, race, physical appearance, language use, stigmas, occupation, and traits (Schneider, 2004). Using these various traits, it is easier for the public to "know" about a certain group of people without actually getting to know them. Stereotyping limited the accurate prediction of cognitive efficiency of many students (McGarthy, 2002). This can be dangerous because such stereotypical thoughts ultimately may affect the decisions made by the teacher regarding a student. Studies agree that teachers who hold stereotypical thoughts tend to produce biased recommendations based on these stereotypical thoughts (Channouf, Mangard, Baudry, & Perney, 2005; Madera, Hebl, & Martin, 2009).

Carman (2011) conducted a mixed-method study where he explored the levels of stereotypical views concerning gifted individuals held by current and future educators. He found that:

> The majority of both levels of teachers held stereotypical thoughts in four of the six areas of stereotypical thoughts examined. Whether in-service or pre-service, stereotypes from each area (gender, ethnicity, age, learning interests, talents, and use of glasses) were held by more than half of the respondents. Some categories (age, ethnicity, and talent) had fewer than 30% of the respondents not holding stereotypical thoughts, with more than 85% of pre-service teachers imagining a Caucasian gifted person. Those holding stereotypical thoughts tend to make biased recommendations based on those stereotypical thoughts. This suggests that the underrepresentation of gifted students from non-majority populations could be related to the nominations given by the teachers. (p. 806)

Equality in placement and accurate identification ensures fair access to gifted services, programs, and many other resources for students. The argument Bracken and Brown (2006) make is that if identification is to be comprehensive, fair, and accessible, then the current method of identifying giftedness needs to be broadened in order to triangulate information from various resources.

3.5.4 Giftedness and Gender

One cannot discuss giftedness without shedding light on important gender differences when it comes to identifying giftedness. Brizendine (2006, 2010) explained that behavior differences between men and women are rooted in biological differences formed before birth; however, male and female brains are more similar than different.

Over time, gifted males and females start to react to their gifted abilities differently. In his study, Swiatek (2001) found that gifted females sometimes denied their giftedness in order to be accepted in their culture. Similarly, gifted girls will "play dumb" due to negative reactions from their peers, their parents, and their environment; gifted girls will also often hide or underestimate themselves. Parents also play a huge role in socializing their daughters to perceived social standards, such as how girls should behave, act, be polite, dress, speak, and so on (Reis & Hébert, 2008). This is not the only problem. According to a study done by Kramer (1985), he found that teachers normally identified more gifted boys than girls and that teachers were usually surprised to find girls who showed extraordinary potential. Sadker and Sadker (1994) drew similar conclusions, when they concluded that "study after study has shown that adults, both teachers and parents, underestimate the intelligence of girls" (as quoted in Reis & Hébert, 2008, p. 283). According to Silverman (1993), misidentifying gifted girls occurs largely because:

> Gifted girls generally have an easier time than gifted boys mastering the complex social skills required of advanced children...gifted girls are much more adept than gifted boys at imitation. They fit in by pretending to be less capable than they really are, disappearing into the crowd. Young gifted girls are rewarded for their compliance and subtly taught to dull their sensibilities and intellectual acumen in the service of social acceptance.... Girls' aptitude for social adaptation often prevents the detection of their giftedness, which, in turn, inhibits the development of their talents. (p. 296)

Many gifted qualities may be present in gifted girls that might be overlooked. For example, leadership, as Silverman (1993) explained, is not promoted as an equal opportunity for males and females. She further explained that leadership skills in males tended to be identified and nurtured, whereas leadership skills in females were often unnoticed or stifled unconsciously.

However, if we focus on academic achievement alone, we find that in scores from the General Certificate in Secondary Education (GCSE), in 2007, 59.1% of girls achieved five or more higher passes compared to 50.6% of boys and 13% of girls scored A or A+ grades in English, compared with 8% of boys (Hymer, 2009).

On the other hand, there is great pressure often with gifted males as well, though regarding different issues. Contrary to females, gifted males are often socialized since birth that males are the providers for the family and that they should always strive for perfection and that, oftentimes and especially, men's careers usually correlate with their masculinity (Hébert, 1991). Therefore, males will end up believing that in order to be a man, they must be "the best" at everything they do, so males will put themselves under a lot of pressure in order to be the best (Reis & Hébert, 2008). A more recent study, however (Kerr & Cohn, 2001), showed that sometimes gifted males will choose athletics over academics, in order to remove the "nerd" label and to increase their masculinity. Thompson (2000) wrote, "Every boy is defined by athletics, whether he likes it or not, whether he is good at them or not" (Reis & Hébert, 2008, p. 270). In addition, gifted boys may also be unidentified due to perceived misbehaviors in class because, unlike gifted girls, gifted boys are not skilled at hiding their abilities (Silverman, 1993). Silverman also explains that gifted boys will often act out in class, by monopolizing the teachers' attention, or by bullying other students for not understanding lessons as fast as he does, or out of sheer boredom, by not being challenged and not being able to identify with anyone in his class. This misbehavior obscures and shadows his talents, and therefore the gifted boy might not be identified as gifted. Thus, as in the case of gifted girls, such gifted boys might not get the attention or service that they need to enhance their giftedness.

The media also plays a huge role in presenting a disparity between the genders. Downes (1994) added that "macho" males and "hero" males are not expected to do well in class, due to media (television, music, etc.) usually portraying males who did poorly in school as heroic underdogs who succeed by other means in life, rather than highlighting already academically successful, gifted boys.

Social pressure and various environmental factors play a huge role in the development of gifted children. Usually, students are socialized since birth toward a stereotypical role in society, so this does not encourage them to be fully themselves or strive to achieve something; the students follow what is stereotypically expected (Reis & Hébert, 2008). Caudill (2006) stated that too much attention is being given to gender inequalities in gifted education, because comparatively, male and female gifted abilities are almost identical. The problem with Caudill's objection and approach is that societies and cultures are teaching different values and expectations to males and females.

3.6 Conclusion

Although the literature on giftedness has expanded, many cultures still adopt the traditional definition of giftedness and the default process of identifying it; teachers still nominate students based on high IQ scores. There seems to be a huge gap between the literature and what is happening on the ground. Not only are the definitions of giftedness unclear, but there are still many cases of underrepresentation of minority populations and students from different socioeconomic backgrounds because of cultural differences, language deficiencies, and social barriers constructed through stereotyping. This is very important. African-American and Hispanic-American students are underrepresented because of their race. White teachers cannot recognize that a student with a background different from their own could be gifted. When a study done by Elhoweris et al. (2005) of 207 elementary school teachers finds a strong association between a students' race or ethnicity and teacher's referrals to gifted programs, cultural factors need to be addressed. Cultural factors are important and need to be factored in when identifying and referring gifted students.

Several methods of identification found in the literature including the SRBCSS, CAB, and others aim to identify gifted students in spite of behavior or language and cultural difficulties. Since such tools exist, are they being used in Lebanon?

Many governments around the world are initiating and developing great educational programs for nurturing gifted students, while others still need a lot of work. In Lebanon and across the Middle East, identification procedures are inconsistently applied, and even standard definitions of "gifted" in several countries are yet to be determined. Among the various identification procedures being used are standardized intelligence tests, creativity tests, achievement tests, rating scales such as the SRBCSS, and attitude surveys; however task commitment is still measured by achievement tests, rating scales, and teacher and parents' judgment. Procedures regarding the identification of gifted children in Lebanon require more examination and further development.

References

Al-Hroub, A. (2010). Developing assessment profiles for mathematically gifted children with learning difficulties at three schools in Cambridgeshire, England. *Journal for the Education of the Gifted, 34*(1), 7–44.

Al-Hroub, A. (2013). Multidimensional model for the identification of gifted children with learning disabilities. *Gifted and Talented International, 28*, 51–69.

Al-Hroub, A. (2014). Identification of dual-exceptional learners. *Procedia-Social and Behavioral Science Journal, 116*, 63–73.

Al-Hroub, A., & Whitebread, D. (2008). Teacher nomination of 'mathematically gifted children with learning difficulties' at three public schools in Jordan. *The British Journal of Special Education, 35*, 152–164.

Assouline, S. G. (2003). Psychological and educational assessment of gifted children. In N. Colangelo & G. Davis (Eds.), *Handbook of gifted education* (3rd ed., pp. 124–145). Boston, MA: Allyn & Bacon.

Bain, S. K., & Bell, S. M. (2004). Social self-concept, social attributions, and peer relationships in fourth, fifth, and sixth graders who are gifted compared to high achievers. *Gifted Child Quarterly, 48*(3), 167–178.

Banaji, M. R., & Greenwald, A. G. (1994). Implicit stereotyping and prejudice. In M. P. Zanna & J. M. Olson (Eds.), *The psychology of prejudice* (pp. 55–76). Hillsdale, NJ: Lawrence Erlbaum.

Bernal, E. M. (2002). Three ways to achieve a more equitable representation of culturally and linguistically different students in GT programs. *Roeper Review, 24*(2), 82–88.

Biernat, M., & Thompson, E. R. (2002). Shifting standards and contextual variation in stereotyping. *European Review of Social Psychology, 12*(1), 103–137.
Binet, A., & Simon, T. (1905a). Methodes nouvelles pour le diagnostic du niveau intellectual des anormaux. *L'Année Psychologique, 11*, 191–244.
Binet, A., & Simon, T. (1905b). Sur la necessité d'établir un diagnostic scientific des états inférieurs de l'intelligence. *L'Année Psychologique, 11*, 163–190.
Bolig, E. E., & Day, J. D. (1993). Dynamic assessment and giftedness: The promise of assessing training responsiveness. *Roeper Review, 16*(2), 110–113.
Bracken, B. A., & Brown, E. F. (2006). Behavioral identification and assessment of gifted and talented students. *Journal of Psychoeducational Assessment, 24*(2), 112–122.
Bracken, B. A., & Keith, L. K. (2004). *CAB, clinical assessment of behavior: Professional manual.* Lutz, FL: PAR, Psychological Assessment Resources.
Brizendine, J. B. (2010). *In their voices: A phenomenological multi-case study related to talent and personal development among gifted and talented young women from five ethnic groups* (Doctoral dissertation, Sam Houston State University).
Brizendine, L. (2006). *The female brain.* New York, NY: Broadway Books.
Burney, V. H., & Beilke, J. R. (2008). The constraints of poverty on high achievement. *Journal for the Education of the Gifted, 31*(3), 295–321.
California Department of Education. (2009a). *State enrollment by ethnicity.* Retrieved from http://dq.cde.ca.gov/dataquest/EnrollEthState.asp?Level=State&TheYear=2007-08&cChoice=EnrollEth1&p=2
California Department of Education. (2009b). *Statewide GATE enrollment.* Retrieved from http://dq.cde.ca.gov/dataquest/Gate1.asp?RptYear=200708&;TheRpt=StGate&cChoice=StGate&cYear=2007-08&cLevel=State&cTopic=Enrollment&myTimeFrame=S
Carman, A. (2011). Stereotypes of giftedness in current and future educators. *Journal for the Education of the Gifted, 34*(5), 790–812.
Caudill, G. (2006). Contemporary issues impacting gifted boys. In B. Wallace & G. Eriksson (Eds.), *Diversity in gifted education* (pp. 200–214). London: Routledge.
Channouf, A., Mangard, C., Baudry, C., & Perney, N. (2005). The effect of salient social stereotypes on academic-tracking decisions. *Revue Européenne de Psychologie Appliqué, 55*(1), 217–223.
Clark, B. (2013). *Growing up gifted: Developing the potential of children at home and at school.* Upper Saddle River, NJ: Pearson Education.
Colangelo, M., & Davis, G. A. (2003). *Handbook of gifted education.* Boston: Allyn and Bacon.
Cotabish, A., Robinson, A., Anthony, T. S., Bryant, L., & Calder-Isgrig, K. (2007). Breaking trends in gifted programs: Increasing representation of culturally diverse and low income students. *Understanding Our Gifted, 20*(1), 21–24.
Coyle, T., Snyder, A., Pillow, D., & Kochunov, P. (2011). SAT predicts GPA better for high ability subjects: Implications for Spearman's law of diminishing. *Personality and Individual Differences, 50*(4), 470–474.
Downes, P. (1994). The gender effect. *Managing Schools Today, 3*(5), 7–8.
Education Trust. (2003). *Education watch: Multiple states. Key education facts and figures. Achievement, attainment and opportunity.* Washington, DC. Retrieved from ERIC database. (ED478501-512.478540-552, 479003-014, 479191, 479209-479221).
Elhoweris, H., Mutua, K., Alsheikh, N., & Holloway, P. (2005). Effect of children's ethnicity on teachers' referral and recommendation decisions in gifted and talent programs. *Remedial and Special Education, 26*(1), 25–31.
Fetzer, E. A. (2000). The gifted/learning-disabled child: A guide for teachers and parents. *Gifted Child Today, 23*(4), 44–50.
Ford, D. Y., Grantham, T. C., & Whiting, G. W. (2008). Culturally and linguistically diverse students in gifted education: Recruitment and retention issues. *Exceptional Children, 74*(3), 289–306.
Ford, D. Y., & Harmon, D. A. (2001). Equity and excellence: Providing access to gifted education for culturally diverse students. *Journal of Secondary Gifted Education, 12*(3), 141–146.

References

Ford, D. Y., & Harmon, D. A. (2002). Equity and excellence: Providing access to gifted education for culturally diverse students. *Journal of Secondary Gifted Education, 12*(1), 141–148.

Freeman, J. (2005). Permission to be gifted: How conceptions of giftedness can change lives. In R. Sternberg & J. Davidson (Eds.), *Conceptions of giftedness* (pp. 80–97). Cambridge: Cambridge University Press.

Gabelko, N. H., & Sosniak, L. A. (2002). 'Someone just like me': When academic engagement trumps race, class, and gender. *Phi Delta Kappan, 83*(5), 400–405.

Galton, F. (1869). *Hereditary genius: An inquiry into its laws and consequences* (Vol. 27). London: Macmillan.

Grantham, T. C. (2002). Underrepresentation in gifted education. *Roeper Review, 24*(1), 50–51.

Grantham, T. C. (2003). Increasing black student enrollment in gifted programs: An exploration of the Pulaski county special school district's advocacy efforts. *Gifted Child Quarterly, 47*(1), 46–65.

Hébert, T. P. (1991). Meeting the affective needs of bright boys through bibliotherapy. *Roeper Review, 13*(1), 207–212.

Heller, K. (2005). The Munich model of giftedness designed to identify and promote gifted students. In R. J. Sternberg & J. E. Davidson (Eds.), *Conceptions of giftedness* (2nd ed., pp. 147–170). New York: Cambridge University Press.

Heller, K. A., & Schofield, N. J. (2008). Identification and nurturing the gifted from an international perspective. In S. I. Pfeiffer (Ed.), *Handbook of giftedness in children* (pp. 93–114). New York: Springer.

Hernández-Torrano, D., & Tursunbayeva, X. (2015). Are teachers biased when nominating students for gifted services? Evidence from Kazakhstan. *High Ability Studies, 5*, 1–13.

Hollingworth, L. S. (1931). The child of very superior intelligence as a special problem in social adjustment. *Mental Hygiene, 15*(1), 3–16.

Hyland, N. E. (2005). Being a good teacher of Black students? White teachers and unintentional racism. *Curriculum Inquiry, 35*(4), 429–459.

Hymer, B. (2009). Understandings and overcoming underachievement in boys. *Able, gifted and talented underachievers, 2*(1), 201–219.

Jarosewich, T., Pfeiffer, S. I., & Morris, J. (2002). Identifying gifted students using teacher rating scales: A review of existing instruments. *Journal of Psychoeducational Assessment, 20*(4), 322–336.

Jenkins, M. D. (1936). A socio-psychological study of Negro children of superior intelligence. *Journal of Negro Education, 5*(2), 175–190.

Kaplan, S., Rodriguez, E., & Siegel, V. (2000). Nontraditional screening. *Communicator, 31*(2), 20–21.

Karnes, F. A., & Stephens, K. R. (2009). Gifted education and legal issues. In L. V. Shavinina (Ed.), *International handbook on giftedness* (pp. 1327–1341). New York: Springer.

Kaufman, A. S., & Kaufman, N. L. (2004a). *Kaufman assessment battery for children* (2nd ed.). Circle Pines, MN: AGS Publishing.

Kaufman, A. S., & Kaufman, N. L. (2004b). *Kaufman test of educational achievement* (2nd ed.). Circle Pines, MN: AGS Publishing.

Kaufman, S. B., & Sternberg, R. J. (2008). Conceptions of giftedness. In S. I. Pfeiffer (Ed.), *Handbook of giftedness in children* (pp. 71–91). New York: Springer.

Kerr, B. A., & Cohn, S. J. (2001). *Smart boys: Talent, manhood, and the search for meaning*. Scottsdale, AZ: Great Potential Press.

Klein, A. G. (2000). Fitting the school to the child: The mission of Leta Stetter Hollingworth, founder of gifted education. *Roeper Review, 23*(2), 97–103.

Kramer, L. R. (1985). *Social interaction and perceptions of ability: A study of gifted adolescent females*. Paper presented at the annual meeting of the American Educational Research Association, Chicago.

Lehman, H. C., & Witty, P. A. (1927). *The psychology of play activities*. Oxford, UK: Barnes.

Lockwood, A. T. (2007). *An agenda for the future: Closing the achievement gap for underrepresented groups in gifted and talented education*. Storrs, CT: National Research Center on the Gifted and Talented.

Lohman, D. F., & Hagen, E. P. (2001). *The cognitive abilities test (Form 6)*. Chicago: Riverside Publishing.

Lupkowski-Shoplik, A., Benbow, C. P., Assouline, S. G., & Brody, L. E. (2003). Talent searches: Meeting the needs of academically talented youth. In N. Colangelo & G. A. Davis (Eds.), *Handbook of gifted education* (3rd ed., pp. 204–218). Boston: Allyn & Bacon.

Madera, J. M., Hebl, M. R., & Martin, R. C. (2009). Gender and letters of recommendation for academia: Agentic and communal differences. *Journal of Applied Psychology, 94*(6), 1591–1599.

Maker, C. J. (2005). *The DISCOVER Project: Improving assessment and curriculum for diverse gifted learners (RM05206)*. Storrs, CT: The National Research Center on the Gifted and Talented.

McBee, M. T. (2006). A descriptive analysis of referral sources for gifted identification screening by race and socioeconomic status. *Journal of Secondary Gifted Education, 17*(2), 103–111.

McCoach, D. B., & Siegle, D. (2007). What predicts teachers' attitudes toward the gifted? *Gifted Child Quarterly, 51*(3), 246–254.

McGarthy, C. (2002). Stereotype formation as category formation. In C. McGarty, V. Y. Yzerbyt, & R. Spears (Eds.), *Stereotypes as explanations* (pp. 16–37). Cambridge, UK: Cambridge University Press.

Minner, S. (1990). Teacher evaluations of case descriptions of LD gifted children. *Gifted Child Quarterly, 34*(1), 37–39.

Moon, S. M. (2003). Personal talent. *High Ability Studies, 14*(1), 5–21.

Moon, S. M. (2007). Counseling issues and research. *Models of counseling gifted children, adolescents, and young adults, 5*(1), 7–27.

Moon, T. R., & Brighton, C. M. (2008). Primary teachers' conceptions of giftedness. *Journal for the Education of the Gifted, 31*(4), 447–480.

Neihart, M., Reis, S., Robinson, N., & Moon, S. M. (Eds.). (2002). *The social and emotional development of gifted children: What do we know?* Waco, TX: Prufrock Press.

Olszewski-Kubilius, P. (2004). Talent searches and accelerated programming for gifted students. In N. Colangelo, S. G. Assouline, & M. Gross (Eds.), *A nation deceived* (Vol. 2, pp. 69–76). Iowa City, IA: University of Iowa.

Otis, A. S., & Lennon, R. T. (1995). *The Otis-Lennon school ability test* (7th ed.). San Antonio: Harcourt Brace Educational Measurement.

Pfeiffer, S. I., & Jarosewich, T. (2003). *Gifted rating scales*. San Antonio, TX: Psychological Corporation.

Reis, S. M., & Hébert, T. P. (2008). Gender and giftedness. In S. I. Pfeiffer (Ed.), *Handbook of giftedness in children* (pp. 271–291). New York: Springer.

Renzulli, J. S. (1990). A practical system for identifying gifted and talented students∗. *Early Child Development and Care, 63*(1), 9–18.

Renzulli, J. S., Smith, L. H., White, A. J., Callahan, C. M., Hartman, R. K., & Westberg, K. L. (1976). *Scales for rating the behavioral characteristics of superior students*. Mansfield Center, CT: Creative Learning Press.

Renzulli, J. S., Smith, L. H., White, A. J., Callahan, C. M., Hartman, R. K., & Westberg, K. L. (2002). *Scales for rating the behavioral characteristics of superior students* (Rev. ed.). Mansfield Center, CT: Creative Learning Press.

Rimm, S., Siegle, D., & Davis, G. (2018). *Education of the gifted and talented* (7th ed.). Boston, MA: Pearson.

Robinson, A., & Clinkenbeard, P. R. (2008). History of giftedness: Perspectives from the past presage modern scholarship. In S. I. Pfeiffer (Ed.), *Handbook of giftedness in children* (pp. 13–31). New York: Springer.

Rohrer, J. C. (1995). Primary teacher conceptions of giftedness: Image, evidence, and nonevidence. *Journal for the Education of the Gifted, 18*(3), 269–283.

Roid, G. H. (2003). *Stanford Binet intelligence scales* (5th ed.). Itasca, IL: Riverside Publishing.

References

Sadker, M., & Sadker, D. (1994). *Failing at fairness: How America's schools cheat girls*. New York: Charles Scribner's Sons.
Sarouphim, K. M., & Maker, C. J. (2010). Ethnic and gender differences in identifying gifted students: A multi-cultural analysis. *International Education, 39*(2), 42.
Schneider, D. J. (2004). *The psychology of stereotyping*. New York, NY: Guilford.
Schroth, S. T., & Helfer, J. A. (2008). Identifying gifted students: Educator beliefs regarding various policies, processes, and procedures. *Journal for the Education of the Gifted, 32*(2), 155–179.
Silverman, L. K. (1993). Social development, leadership, and gender issues. In *Counseling the gifted and talented* (pp. 291–327). Denver: Love.
Speirs, K. L., Neumeister, K. L., Adams, C. M., Pierce, R. L., Cassady, J. C., & Dixon, F. A. (2007). Fourth-grade teachers' perceptions of giftedness: Implications for identifying and serving diverse gifted students. *Journal for the Education of the Gifted, 30*(4), 479–499.
Subhi-Yamin, T. (1992). *Giftedness and creativity: The computerized comprehensive identification procedure*. Amman/Jordan: Scientific Enlightenment Publishing House.
Subhi-Yamin, T. (2009). Gifted education in the Arabian gulf and the middle eastern regions: History, current practices, new directions, and future trends. In L. V. Shavinina (Ed.), *International handbook on giftedness* (pp. 1463–1490). New York: Springer.
Swiatek, M. A. (2001). Social coping among gifted high school students and its relationship to self-concept. *Journal of Youth and Adolescence, 30*(1), 19–39.
Tannenbaum, A. J. (1979). Pre-Sputnik to post-Watergate concern about the gifted. In A. H. Passow (Ed.), *The gifted and the talented* (pp. 5–27). Chicago: National Society for the Study of Education.
Terman, L. M. (1954). The discovery and encouragement of exceptional talent. *American Psychologist, 9*(6), 221–226.
Thompson, M. (2000). *Speaking of boys: Answers to the most-asked questions about raising sons*. New York: Ballantine Books.
Thompson, M. (2001). *The psychology of dyslexia: A handbook for teachers*. Londin, UK: Whurr.
Torrance, E. P. (1970). *Torrance tests of creative thinking*. Lexington, MA: Personal Press.
Tyler, K. M., Boykin, A. W., & Walton, T. R. (2006). Cultural considerations. *Teaching and Teacher Education, 22*(8), 998–1005.
Vygotsky, L. (1983). *The history of higher mental functions. In collected works* (Vol. 3). Moscow: Pedagogika (in Russian, written in 1931).
Wechsler, D. (2003). *Wechsler intelligence scale for children* (4th ed.). San Antonio, TX: The Psychological Corporation.
Witty, P. A. (1930). A study of one hundred gifted children. *University of Kansas Bulletin of Education, 2*(8), 3–44.
Witty, P. A., & Jenkins, M. D. (1934). The educational achievement of a group of gifted Negro children. *Journal of Educational Psychology, 25*(8), 585–597.
Witty, P. A., & Jenkins, M. D. (1935). The case of 'B'—A gifted Negro girl. *Journal of Social sychology, 6*(1), 117–124.
Wu, S. C., & Elliott, R. T. (2008). A study of reward preference in Taiwanese gifted and nongifted students with differential locus of control. *Journal for the Education of the Gifted, 32*(2), 230–244.
Yoon, S. Y., & Gentry, M. (2009). Racial and ethnic representation in gifted programs. *Gifted Child Quarterly, 53*(2), 121–136.
Ziegler, A., & Heller, K. A. (2003). Attribution retraining with gifted girls. *Roeper Review, 23*(1), 217–248.
Ziegler, A., & Stoeger, H. (2003). Identification of underachievement: An empirical study on the agreement among various diagnostic sources. *Gifted and Talented International, 18*(1), 87–94.

Chapter 4
Researching Teachers' Perceptions and Procedures for Identification of Giftedness in Lebanon

Sara El Khoury and Anies Al-Hroub

Abstract This research adopted a mixed research design in order to explore current elementary teachers' perceptions concerning the attributes of gifted students as a starting point in order to locate the lack of understanding in the construct of giftedness. The purpose of this study was twofold: (1) to explore the perceptions teachers currently have concerning the attributes of gifted students and (2) to survey the current practices used as the means for identifying gifted students. The data were collected through 140 surveys administered in 6 schools, 15 semi-structured interviews, and 5 focus group discussions with elementary school teachers in 5 private schools in the greater Beirut area. This chapter incorporates the research questions guiding the study, together with a description of the adopted research design, method, population, participants, and selection process. In addition, a description is included of the data collection methods that were used, the tools, and the data analysis procedures.

4.1 Purpose of the Study

There is a strong trend in educational research nowadays particularly on special educational programs in schools across Lebanon. These services usually include catering for students with intellectual disabilities, physical disabilities, and other types of disabilities. However, there seems to be a lack of services for, and research on, students who are gifted (Sarouphim, 2010). Very few research studies were extracted regarding gifted students in Lebanon in contrast to studies

---

Sara El Khoury (✉)
Department of Education, American University of Beirut, Jounieh, Lebanon
e-mail: sie07@aub.edu.lb

Anies Al-Hroub
Department of Education, Chairperson, American University of Beirut, Beirut, Lebanon
e-mail: aa111@aub.edu.lb

pertaining to students with disabilities. The purpose of this study was to investigate and explore the current understanding and conception of giftedness on the part of teachers in Lebanese schools. In addition, it explored current identification procedures. Hence, our aims were twofold: (a) to explore the perceptions that teachers currently have of the attributes and characteristics of gifted students in Lebanese schools and (b) to survey the current school practices used to identify gifted students.

4.2 Research Questions

The research questions guiding this study are: (a) What are Lebanese private elementary school teachers' conceptions of the attributes of gifted students? (b) What are the current practices used to identify gifted students?

4.3 Research Design

This study adopted a mixed-method approach that explored the aims of the research through a combination of quantitative and qualitative measures. Gall, Gall, and Borg (2006) define mixed-method research studies as "a type of study that uses both quantitative and qualitative techniques for data collection and analysis, either concurrently or sequentially, to address the same or related research questions" (p. 461). The bulk of this research adopted a qualitative research design because of its focus on individual understandings or conceptions (Lee, 2006).

One of the aims was to explore teachers' perceptions on the attributes of gifted students. Consequently, we used qualitative measures to survey the current practices used to identify gifted students. Finally, qualitative and quantitative measures were used to identify the characteristics that teachers focus on when identifying gifted students.

4.4 Study Site

We conducted the study in six private schools in the Greater Beirut Area. This study initially concentrated on five schools, but in order to reach our target of 150 surveys, we distributed the surveys to a sixth private school. We conducted focus group discussions and interviews in the original five schools that were the focus of the study. These schools are bilingual with English and Arabic subjects at the elementary school level. All schools in this study provide classes from nursery to grade 12. One accommodates more than 1200 students who attend classes from

Table 4.1 Composition of sample by gender and school

Method	Gender	School 1	School 2	School 3	School 4	School 5	School 6	Total
Surveys	Male	1	2	4	2	3	0	12
	Female	15	19	20	18	32	24	128
	Total	16	21	24	20	35	24	**140**
FGDs	Male	3	4	2	3	1	–	13
	Female	5	5	10	9	9	–	38
	Total	8	9	12	12	10	–	**51**
Interviews	Male	0	0	1	1	1	–	3
	Female	3	3	2	2	2	–	12
	Total	3	3	3	3	3	–	**15**

nursery to grade 12, and the other four had between 600 and 1200 students. Two of the schools implement the IB (International Baccalaureate), and all of the schools in this study enrich students' knowledge of languages by teaching French as a second foreign language, starting from grade 1. Physically the schools were fairly typical; one school, for example, is a five-story building built in the early 1960s, serving children from kindergarten to grade 4, and all with their own libraries, computer centers, and auditoria administration blocks and adjacent to the buildings, playgrounds, as well as music rooms and cafeterias. In addition, all of these schools have "special support personnel," as one school terms it, who provides special educational services to students with special needs.

4.5 Method

4.5.1 Participants

One hundred fifty (150) survey forms were distributed to elementary private school teachers in six schools, and 140 completed surveys in total were returned. The respondents to the surveys and participants in the interviews and focus group discussions consisted of elementary private school teachers who had agreed to participate in the study. As for selecting key informants, we chose individuals who were directly involved with the students and who were classroom teachers. The researchers used purposeful sampling to include male and female elementary teachers of different subjects (e.g., mathematics, science, English). Participation in this study was voluntary, and out of those teachers who completed the survey, three from each school – a total of 15 teachers – volunteered to participate in the interviews. In addition, between 8 and 12 teachers took part in each of the five focus group discussions (FGDs). Table 4.1 illustrates the number of male and female teachers who completed the surveys and participated in the FGDs and interviews.

4.6 Data Collection

We used three data collection tools in this research. Triangulation of the results was conducted using data obtained from the informal, open-ended, semi-structured interviews, the focus group discussions, and the written surveys. The surveys were used to collect the age of participants; their teaching experience; information about whether they had ever encountered a gifted student in their class and, if yes, whether this student was male or female; and so on. The interviews and focus groups were audio-taped. Another interviewer was present during the focus group discussions in order to allow comparison of notes. Interviews and FDGs were conducted because we believed that by speaking directly to the stakeholders (i.e., the teachers) involved in the day-to-day life of the school, they would provide a clearer picture of the issues involved in the decision to refer a student for a place in the gifted program and on what basis. The language used in the surveys and the language of communication in the semi-structured interviews and FGDs were English. Below is a description of the advantages and disadvantages of each tool and the rationale for using these tools in the present study.

4.6.1 Perceptions of Giftedness Survey

The survey used is entitled the "Perceptions of Giftedness Survey." According to Kelley, Clark, Brown, and Sitzia (2003), the term "survey" is defined as:

> The selection of a relatively large sample of people from a pre-determined population (the 'population of interest'; this is the wide group of people in whom the researcher is interested in a particular study), followed by the collection of a relatively small amount of data from those individuals. One important element to consider with surveys is that they are designed to provide a "snapshot of how things are at a specific time". (p. 261)

Major changes are taking place in survey research. Although web surveys provide a time- and cost-saving option for data collection (Dillman, 2000), paper and pencil surveys were used instead in this study, for several reasons. One was that some individuals might not have had web access readily available to them (Umbach, 2004) (the case in Lebanon), thereby hindering or preventing them from completing the survey. Another reason was that because completion of an online survey was not given a completion deadline, the process of receiving returns might have taken a long time (Sax, Gilmartin & Bryant, 2003). In their study, Sax et al. (2003) concluded, "across the four modes of administration, response rates were highest among students who received a paper survey, with the option to complete the survey online" (p. 423). Sax et al. also mentioned that the generalizability of data collected online is less feasible than that of those obtained from paper and pencil surveys. Finally, limited access to the Internet, difficulties in ensuring anonymity and confidentiality, and technical problems all present other problems (Sax et al. 2003). Therefore, paper-pencil surveys were used in this study.

There are several advantages for using surveys: one advantage in this study was the fact that the data were obtained based on real-world observations and empirical data (Kelley, et al., 2003). Another advantage of using surveys is that we can cover a wide range of people and events, and this means that it is more likely that the data obtained will be based on a representative sample and can therefore be generalized to a population. Lastly, surveys can produce a large amount of data within a short time at a fairly low cost. As a result, the researcher can set a limit to the period for the data collection, and this can assist with the planning and delivery of the results (Kelley et al., 2003). The purpose behind using surveys in this study was to gather information about the participants' characteristics, university degrees, years of experience, and so on. The surveys helped to elicit general responses to our research questions so that the responses could be examined in more detail in the focus group discussions and interviews.

As well as advantages, surveys can also carry several disadvantages, namely, that the significance of the data may be overlooked if the researcher focuses too much on the range of coverage to the exclusion of taking adequate account of the implications of that data for relevant issues, problems, and theories. For example, in this study only teachers filled out the surveys, leaving out the special educators, counselors, and other key professionals who could have been important in identifying gifted students in the classroom. Another disadvantage more specific to this study was that the data produced from the surveys alone would have lacked sufficient detail and depth with respect to our topic. This is why focus group discussions and interviews were included as data collection tools. Since this study was about perceptions, surveys alone would not have been sufficient to measure these (Kelley et al., 2003). Though this is a controversial issue, this study adopted the paper and pencil survey instead of using a web-based method due to its speed in obtaining results.

4.6.2 Focus Group Discussions

Although surveys and interviews are common methods for gathering data, focus group discussions (FDGs) have become increasingly popular as well, especially in qualitative research. The FGD is a dynamic form of assessment, a semi-structured data-gathering method in which a purposively selected set of participants gather to discuss issues and concerns based on a list of key themes drawn up by the moderator/facilitator (Hennink, 2013). Because the study was mainly concerned with exploring teachers' conceptions, it was considered appropriate to include a focus group discussion in the methodology to allow a more in-depth analysis and discussion of how teachers perceive and recognize gifted students in Lebanese schools. The FDGs were conducted at the schools where the participants were teaching, at a convenient time following consultation with school principals. The number of participants in each FGD was between 8 and 12 female and male teachers, and the duration of the discussions was between 90 and 120 min. The bulk of the FGD was devoted to the discussion of the different themes, and the remaining time was dedicated to introductions, the wrap-up, and so on. The themes that were discussed were teachers' cultural understandings of the attributes of giftedness, their perceptions of the prevalence of giftedness, teachers' recommendations with regard to identifying and defining gifted students, the services and programs that are already available (and of which the teachers are aware), and their recommendations for further programs.

FGDs were used in this study as one of their main advantages is that the dialogue between the participants takes on a life of its own. The discussion takes place within a group forum, and participants tend to "piggyback" onto each other's comments which adds richness to the discussion (Hennink, 2013). Other advantages include efficiency; this is because it is possible to obtain the views of a number of people at the same time. More importantly, participants frequently express views that they might not otherwise articulate in other settings, and responses are often spontaneous in nature. For example, when discussing identification procedures, each teacher had his/her own method, and so this added richness to the discussion. Flexibility is an advantage as well, as the facilitator is able to probe for clarification or for extra detail. Another benefit is that FGDs generally work well with a range of populations, including, participants with low self-esteem or those who lack experience in expressing their personal views. Some teachers might have been relieved to discover they were not the only ones who had to deal with identifying a gifted student and thus might have felt encouraged to share their experiences. Finally, and most importantly, the whole aim and function of the FGD is to gather information about the opinions and perceptions of the group members (Hennink, 2013), which was the precise purpose of this study. Therefore, the FGD was appropriate for exploring teachers' perceptions of the attributes of giftedness and our other research questions. As previously mentioned, giftedness can be found in all cultures and is expressed through a variety of behaviors (Baldwin, 2005). What sort of behaviors do Lebanese teachers look for in their students in order to identify them as gifted? Consequently, identifying gifted students from culturally diverse groups was an important issue. The FGDs helped to explore Lebanese teachers' understandings and conceptions of giftedness.

However, there are some disadvantages to using FGDs, one of which is that the success of the discussion depends greatly on the skill of the moderator in terms of how they are able to stimulate and manage the group discussion and whether they can ensure that the discussion flows freely. This is why another person was present alongside the researcher during the discussion. Another problem that had to be overcome was the difficulty of assembling the groups, as the participants had to give up their time to take part in the discussion. Finding a common time for all to meet was also an issue. It is important for the researcher to provide a comfortable, secure, and relaxing atmosphere. A further major disadvantage of FGDs is that each individual response may not be independent of the other responses, and the group dynamic may vary significantly.

Unlike interviews, the moderator in FGDs has less control over the discussion. For example, there may be some form of pressure in the group to conform to the group "norm," and therefore many important opinions may not be expressed.

Finally, the participants are not randomly selected so findings are not generalizable (Hennink, 2013).

4.6.3 Semi-Structured Interviews

The purpose of conducting interviews is to "gather descriptions of the life-world of the interviewee with respect to interpretation of the meaning of the described phenomena" (Creswell, Clark, Gutmann, & Hanson, 2003, p.11). According to Creswell et al., there are three types of interviews: unstructured, semi-structured, and structured. Unstructured interviews provide:

> A broad purpose statement that is used in lieu of a guide; respondents determine subject matter. Semi-structured interviews have topic areas, which are used to form a discussion guide outline, yet no specific questions are included. Structured interviews have a defined set of questions (or guidelines) used to guide the discussion. (p. 6)

For this study, we used semi-structured interviews, with open-ended questions, because they allowed participants to provide answers representing different viewpoints and they gave participants opportunities to express their thoughts, feelings, and perceptions based on their specific situations. Individual interviews can often provide in-depth information about the context and participants' stories, and they can allow the discussion to range across one or more topics. This is why we chose to conduct interviews in this study. Although face-to-face interviews are more costly and time-consuming methods than carrying out surveys, the researcher can select the sample of participants (in this case, male and female elementary school teachers, teaching different subjects and with different lengths of experience) to balance the demographic profile of the sample (Kelley et al., 2003). There are many advantages and disadvantages pertaining to conducting interviews.

Interviews generally allow for focused discussions and follow-up questions. In addition, some participants may offer more information in interviews than they would in a group context. They may feel more comfortable discussing issues on a one-to-one basis with the researcher and may include more recommendations and contribute more insights than discussing the issues in front of their peers. Furthermore, interviews are usually a great source of stories and information about the context. More importantly, the interviewer can observe the non-verbal behaviors of the interviewee. At the practical level, an important advantage is that interviews allow more flexibility in relation to location, scheduling, and the range of topics for discussion than FGDs (Creswell, et al., 2003). Another important advantage of individual interviews over FGDs is that the structure of interviews helps to overcome the problem of interpersonal group dynamics influencing responses through group pressure or group domination by a strong and persuasive individual (Creswell, et al., 2003). Finally, some individuals may appreciate the additional personal attention that the interview can offer and which is lacking in FGDs or surveys.

Although conducting individual interviews has many advantages, there are some disadvantages, including the time commitment required of both interviewers and interviewees, which can be significant, especially for teachers who have children. Furthermore, there is the issue of sensitivity, in which participants may have some personal issues that they may not want to discuss with the interviewer (Creswell, et al., 2003). Finally, there is a matter of access to dangerous or politically sensitive sites (as can be the case in Lebanon) which may be difficult to reach and requires careful handling.

However, in the present study, the advantages outweighed the disadvantages, so interviews were part of our data collection procedure. In order to obtain comprehensive results, all three methods discussed above were included in the process of data collection, thereby eliminating the individual disadvantages of each method. As already mentioned, triangulation of our results was possible because FGDs were held, followed by separate interviews with each participant, using informal, open-ended, semi-structured questions, with surveys used to back up the responses. Triangulation was important because data were collected from more than one source; therefore consistency and validity were achieved.

4.7 Design of the Three Data Collection Tools

4.7.1 The Survey

The survey that was used was a compilation of that used by Neumeister, Adam, Pierce, Cassady, and Dixon (2007) in their study entitled *Fourth-grade teachers' perceptions of giftedness: implications for identifying and serving diverse gifted students* and the one employed by Lee (2006) in the study entitled *Teachers' conceptions of gifted and talented young children*. In our survey, we modified some of the characteristics listed in the above surveys to fit our purposes. For example, we removed the frequency section in Neumeister et al.'s survey, and we made several additions to Lee's survey, removing unnecessary redundant items.

The survey was divided into three parts: (1) personal information, (2) conceptions and definitions of giftedness (teachers' beliefs about the meaning and manifestation of giftedness), and (3) characteristics and prevalence (teachers' beliefs about which characteristics should be considered the most important in identifying gifted students). The first part of the survey consists of general information about the individual teacher completing the survey, including their length of experience, grades that they taught, their level of education, and so on. In the second and the last part of the survey, teachers indicated the likelihood of identifying a student as gifted if that student exhibited the characteristics that were listed, by circling the number corresponding to their response. There were two final questions asking the participant if he/she would like to participate in the FGD and the interview.

4.7.2 Focus Group Discussion and Semi-Structured Interviews

Because the study was mainly about exploring teachers' conceptions, it was appropriate to include FGDs and semi-structured interviews in the methodology in order to obtain a more in-depth picture of how teachers perceive and recognize gifted students in Lebanese schools. These two methods helped reveal the teachers' perceptions in detail as the teachers spoke directly about their opinions and rationales to a greater extent than they were able to express in the survey. The bulk of the interview involved the discussion of the different themes, and the remaining time was dedicated to introductions, a brief icebreaker, and the wrap-up. Several participants offered more information in the interviews than they did in a group context.

The discussions in the FGDs and interviews moved from general to specific topics and focused on relevant issues. Once introductions had been made and the aims of the interviews had been clarified, the discussion moved through three stages: (1) definition and concepts, (2) characteristics and prevalence, and (3) means of identification. "Definition and concepts" pertained to the first research question; characteristics and attributes and means of identification are related to the second research question. Although the second and third parts of the interviews might seem similar, there were some major differences between them. To explain, the second part of the interviews focused more on prevalence and identifying gifted students and talking about the students in general, whereas in the third part of the interviews, the discussion was more specific, with teachers being expected to provide specific examples and recommendations.

4.8 Data Collection Procedure

In order for our results to be more comprehensive and valid, the data collection took place in six different private schools. We contacted ten private schools, but only six schools were interested to participate in this study. Of those six schools, five accepted to be involved in both the interviews and FGDs, and one school was only interested in completing the surveys. In order to reach our 150 survey target, we sent our surveys to the 6 interested schools, distributing 30 surveys per school. Overall, we received 140 completed surveys out of the 150 we distributed. There was a question at the end of the survey, which inquired whether the respondent would like to participate in the FGD and the interview, and the participant ticked either "Yes" or "No." For those who responded with a "Yes," a letter of invitation was sent to each individual participant around 1–2 weeks before the session. A reminder was also sent 1 day before the session. Nametags were distributed among the participants to encourage friendliness and ease among the group. Following the FGDs, 1-h interviews were conducted with three elementary teachers per school, who were randomly chosen from the teachers who had agreed to participate in the study, and the selection took into consideration the teacher's background and experience.

In order to keep track during the FGD and interview sessions, while at the same time allowing the participants to discuss freely and spontaneously, the facilitator used a discussion guide that listed the main themes to be covered in the session. This list of themes was kept to a minimum in order to leave enough time for insightful and in-depth discussion. Unlike the semi-structured interviews, the FGD moderator has less control over the discussion. Moreover, in this study, the participants were not randomly sampled, so findings are not generalizable (Hennink, 2013).

4.9 Data Analysis

The mode of data analysis chosen was interpretational analysis. It consisted of the following steps: firstly, we recorded all the data that we had collected from our interviews and focus groups. Then we had to break down the texts into segments. After that, we defined specific categories (or themes) in order to reflect each important conceptual element that appeared. Next, we coded each segment for all the categories that applied to that segment. Once we had placed all the data segments into categories, we compared each code across the segments in order to explore and discover commonalities in the data that reflected the underlying meaning of, and/or the relationship among, the coding categories. This helped us interpret our data in order to highlight the common conceptions and misconceptions that the teachers held pertaining to the attributes of gifted students.

4.10 Trustworthiness of Results

Schwandt (2001) defined trustworthiness as "that quality of an investigation (and its findings) that made it noteworthy to audiences" (p. 258). Hence, the trustworthiness criteria consist of ensuring the (1) credibility, (2) transferability, (3) dependability, and (4) conformability of the research being conducted (Schwandt, 2001).

Credibility (or internal validity) is the degree to which the researcher understands and represents the participants' perceptions accurately (Schwandt, 2001). This can be attained by (1) triangulation, (2) member checks, (3) long-term observation, (4) peer examination, (5) participatory or collaborative modes of research, and (6) the researcher's biases (Merriam, 2007). However, for the purpose of this research, only triangulation, member checks, and research bias were used. With regard to triangulation, we conducted FGDs in each school and then interviewed individual participants separately. We used surveys as well to check whether there was consistency in the answers. Member checks were carried out at the end of each interview by summarizing the participants' answers. This gave the participants a chance to comment on what they said in order to maintain accuracy. The researchers' bias and theoretical orientation were not included in the study.

Moving on to transferability (or external validity) or the extent to which the findings of the study are generalizable to contexts beyond those in which the study was conducted (Schwandt, 2001), in this study, we provided an in-depth description of the history, setting, participants, and culture of the schools and research participants, in order to facilitate the transferability of the findings. However, it should be noted that due to the limited scope of this study (only teachers in the private elementary school sphere were studied), this presents a limitation to the transferability of the results. We encourage more research to be done on a larger scale in the future.

Dependability (or in other words reliability) is the extent to which this process is "logical, traceable, and documented" (Schwandt, 2001, p. 258). This was assured in two ways. First, regarding the researcher's position, the researcher provided a description of the underlying assumptions and theories behind the study but gave no evidence of their personal opinions to the study. Moreover, an audit trial was made, in which the study provided a detailed description about how the data was collected and how the researcher later constructed themes and categories (Merriam, 2007).

Finally, conformability is the degree of accuracy concerning the data collected without the researcher's bias. This was done in two ways: by triangulation of the results and by the audit trial (both were discussed above). Hence, in order to ensure our trustworthiness of results, this study implemented the following strategies: (1) triangulation, (2) member checks, (3) rich and thick description, (4) multisite design, (5) the researcher's position, and (8) audit trial.

There are no common procedures or criteria for detecting or recognizing gifted students in Lebanon, and it is for this reason that this study may be considered useful. No previous studies have been conducted addressing these issues. It may help policy-makers to make use of the results in order to derive a plan to help identify students who are gifted. We also included quantitative data used to identify the number of schools that provide special educational services and whether or not they have acceleration programs or indeed *any* program for gifted students. In order to test the chain of events, we kept a written record documenting all the procedures used in the data collection and analysis. This was designed to ensure that other researchers would be able to use the same methodology and replicate the study.

References

Baldwin, A. Y. (2005). Identification concerns for gifted students of diverse populations. *Theory into Practice, 44*(2), 105–114.

Creswell, J. W., Plano Clark, V. L., Gutmann, M. L., & Hanson, W. E. (2003). Advanced mixed methods research designs. In A. Tashakkori & C. Teddlie (Eds.), *Handbook on mixed methods in the behavioral and social sciences* (pp. 209–240). Thousand Oaks, CA: Sage Publications.

Dillman, D. A. (2000). *Mail and internet surveys: The tailor design method* (2nd ed.). New York, NY: Wiley.

Gall, M. D., Gall, J. P., & Borg, W. R. (2006). *Educational research: An introduction*. New York, NY: Pearson Education.

Hennink, M. M. (2013). *Understanding focus group discussions*. New York, NY: Oxford University Press.
Kelley, K., Clark, B., Brown, V., & Sitzia, J. (2003). Good practice in the conduct and reporting of survey research. *International Journal for Quality in Health Care., 15*(3), 261–266.
Lee, L. (2006). Teachers' conceptions of gifted and talented young children. *High Ability Studies, 10*(3), 183–196.
Merriam, S. B. (2007). *Qualitative research and case study applications in education: Revised and expanded from case study research in education*. San Francisco, CA: Jossey-Bass Publishers.
Neumeister, K. L. S., Adams, C. M., Pierce, R. L., Cassady, J. C., & Dixon, F. A. (2007). Fourth-grade teachers' perceptions of giftedness: Implications for identifying and serving diverse gifted students. *Journal for the Education of the Gifted, 30*(4), 479–499.
Sarouphim, K. M. (2010). A model for the education of gifted learners in Lebanon. *International Journal of Special Education, 25*(1), 71–79.
Sax, L. J., Gilmartin, S. K., & Bryant, A. N. (2003). Assessing response rates and nonresponse bias in web and paper surveys. *Research in Higher Education, 44*(4), 409–432.
Schwandt, T. A. (2001). *Dictionary of qualitative inquiry* (2nd ed.). Thousand Oaks, CA: Sage.
Umbach, P. D. (2004). Web surveys: Best practices. *New Directions for Institutional Research, 121*, 23–38.

Chapter 5
Defining and Identifying Giftedness in Lebanon: Findings from the Field

Sara El Khoury and Anies Al-Hroub

Abstract The research findings in this chapter are divided into three parts. The first part concentrates on the various definitions of giftedness that surfaced from the 15 interviews and 5 focus group discussions (FGDs), collaborated by the 140 survey results. The second part focuses on the different perceived attributes and characteristics that the teachers felt gifted students exhibit, which emerged during the interviews and FGDs. The third part focuses on the identification procedures used by the various teachers. The results of this study are thematically presented, and each section is a combination of the survey results, semi-structured interviews, and the focus group discussions. To maintain the confidentially of the data provided by participants, all names used below are pseudonyms.

5.1 Introduction

The first section pertains to the various responses with regard to perceptions of definitions of giftedness. Each teacher was asked simply to define what giftedness meant to them, and then they were asked to come up with a definition that was specifically relevant to the Lebanese educational context. In the FGDs and interviews, teachers gave several definitions, together with some recommendations. There is no unified Lebanese definition because the Ministry of Education and Higher Education (MEHE) does not have a policy on serving gifted and

---

Sara El Khoury (✉)
Department of Education, American University of Beirut, Jounieh, Lebanon
e-mail: sie07@aub.edu.lb

Anies Al-Hroub
Department of Education, Chairperson, American University of Beirut, Beirut, Lebanon
e-mail: aa111@aub.edu.lb

© The Author(s), under exclusive licence to Springer International Publishing
AG, part of Springer Nature 2018
S. El Khoury, A. Al-Hroub, *Gifted Education in Lebanese Schools*,
SpringerBriefs in Psychology, https://doi.org/10.1007/978-3-319-78592-9_5

talented children and adolescents at schools. Teachers' constructs of how schools and society understand and practice giftedness are based almost purely on their own practice. Therefore, the definitions and attributes listed in the following sections have arisen from the Lebanese teachers' own personal understanding and beliefs that have accumulated through practice. The second section describes all the main characteristics that surfaced during the interviews and FGDs. The last section portrays the different responses about identification procedures that are perceived by the teachers.

5.2 Definitions of Giftedness

The responses of the semi-structured interviews and FGDs were categorized according to the following themes: what creates or is the nature of giftedness and the subthemes surrounding high intellectual ability, high academic performance, social intelligence, leadership, and creativity. Although leadership and creativity were not specifically mentioned as defining attributes, they were cited in almost every interview and FGD as two of the most important characteristics that define a gifted student, which is the reason they have been treated equally in this section.

Even though there are some internationally accepted definitions, there is no consensus or agreement on one definition in Lebanon: cultural factors make it difficult to achieve this. Our aim was to discover a culturally specific definition.

5.2.1 What Creates Giftedness?

Two main beliefs emerged about how giftedness is created, and this was an issue of debate among several teachers. Some believed that children are born gifted, while others considered that the environment plays a more crucial role. Several teachers used the term "God given" or "God-given intelligence." Christina who teaches mathematics said, "Giftedness is something God-given. It is an innate quality and makes that student smarter, faster, giving them the ability to ask more intelligent questions than the other students." Similarly, Rania who is a homeroom teacher said, "Giftedness is something that is innate... I would say.... Something that a child has... You cannot teach a child to be gifted, it is something within them." The teachers who referred to "God-given" intelligence assumed that giftedness is created before birth and the environment has little to do with the origin of giftedness.

Some teachers who expressed the above belief also included the importance of nurturing this God-given giftedness. For example, Raghida, an English teacher said, "Society helps nurture one's giftedness." During the FGD in School 2, Maria, a homeroom teacher, added that teachers should be able to "get the giftedness out of them." Similarly, during the FGD in another school, Susan,

5.2 Definitions of Giftedness

also a homeroom teacher, stated, "We need to keep on developing the student's giftedness; otherwise it will freeze at a certain point." Nour, a mathematics teacher, said:

> Now maybe we can develop his [or her] skills more, and if he [or she] is outstanding in a subject, let us say in English, we can work harder on developing these skills, because maybe he's going to end up being a very important author later, or a journalist. So you develop these things.

These responses indicate the importance of nurturing giftedness and that it is not enough for the child to be born with exceptional abilities.

5.2.2 High Intellectual Ability

Some teachers used the terms intelligence and giftedness interchangeably. Based on contemporary broad definitions of giftedness, this was equivocal, as they are two very distinct concepts. A science teacher, Lina, stated, "In order for a student to be classified as gifted, no matter what he does or what his ambition is, having a very high IQ score is a determinant of identifying him as gifted." Most teachers still believe that having a high IQ score is what determines whether a student is gifted or not. For many teachers in this study, high intellectual ability meant having a high IQ. Two teachers in two of the interviews said that talent or aptitude in a student, but without very high intellectual ability, does not define the student as gifted. Hiba, a science teacher said, "I'm basing my gifted students on the IQ test."

Similarly, four teachers discussed how teachers in Lebanon believed that the higher the IQ, the more gifted the student is. Nour, a mathematics teacher, surmised:

> I would have to say that high IQ scores are definitely relevant to the Lebanese context. How else would we know? We don't have any other standardized test that I know of to test his level of giftedness.

Another point made during the FGDs in two schools was that a high IQ should not necessarily be the only criterion for determining giftedness. One teacher said, "So what if he has a high IQ? ....Many people have a high IQ, but cannot construct a proper sentence, or stutter, or are not good in social situations. To me, this is ridiculous." In one of the FGDs, one science teacher commented, "High IQ! But maybe they have a brilliant IQ score, but are not very gifted in class. So it's not relevant."

Only one teacher mentioned that the gifted student should be logical. Yasmina, a homeroom teacher, talked about how a student must have high logical thinking skills to be considered gifted. She said, "He must be logical in his answers and his questions, and in his thinking." Logical thinking (finding/providing a solution) corresponds to academic intelligence. One teacher referred to it as "the ability to think logically," and some teachers emphasized it, when they referred to terms such as "academic intelligence" or "IQ."

5.2.3 High Academic Performance

High academic performance means achieving high grades. Teachers in this study had different views concerning which subjects were more important when it came to identifying giftedness in students. The results here are divided into four categories: (1) gifted in only one subject area, (2) gifted in all subject areas, (3) gifted only in the sciences (the "medical doctor or engineer" syndrome), and (4) multiple areas of giftedness.

When asked to provide a definition of giftedness, 5 out of the 15 interviewees mentioned characteristics related to "high academic performance." Caroline, a homeroom teacher, stated:

> …somebody who is advanced compared to his [or her] classmates, and somebody who is able, maybe, to understand the lesson, maybe from the first time. Sometimes before you start talking, if you only write the title on the board, they are able to understand what you are going to talk about. I notice this about them.

Ibrahim, a mathematics teacher, explained that the Lebanese perception of the gifted child was "someone who gets high grades." However, Ibrahim believed that high academic performance does not necessarily mean high grades. He made it clear that a definition of giftedness based on high school grades is a narrow definition. He explained, "In my opinion, a gifted student is someone who shines in his own way in the field that he is best at."

Four teachers mentioned that it is enough for a child to excel in one school subject for that child to be considered gifted. Hiba, a science teacher, said, "Giftedness could be in one area or in one subject, like calculation in math maybe, not [necessarily] so good in writing an essay, or in answering comprehension questions or vice versa." Ahmad, also a science teacher, said, "The student should be gifted in one subject. He will be excellent in it." This group of teachers believed that a student who is gifted would be expected to excel in at least one subject.

On the other hand, many teachers believed that a gifted student might be expected to be outstanding in all subjects. One example was when Nour, a mathematics teacher, explained, "I feel that a gifted student has to be smart in everything. I'm not just specifying only in math or in English, it has to be in all."

Yasmina, a homeroom teacher, likewise stated that a gifted student should not exhibit excellence in only one subject but should demonstrate superiority in all subjects of the Lebanese curriculum because it is "the most difficult curriculum in my opinion." She added:

> Because the Lebanese curriculum is more difficult than other curricula, so a gifted student should be able to excel in it, and excel higher than his [grade] level. He knows more. He grasps things quickly, from books, T.V., etc. He knows too much. He should excel in all subjects.

Therefore, some teachers believed that in order to classify a student as truly gifted, he/she must be outstanding in all subject areas, whether included in the Lebanese curriculum or another one.

5.2 Definitions of Giftedness

Three mathematics teachers, two science teachers, and one homeroom teacher mentioned the importance of high achievement, mainly in relation to scientific subjects, namely, mathematics and the sciences. If a student excelled in subjects like language arts, physical education (PE), and the arts, he/she might be "talented" or "good" at this subject, but this did not mean they were "gifted." In fact, one mathematics teacher, Fatima, specifically mentioned that if a student is excellent at English, for example, then he/she would not necessarily be considered gifted. She added:

> Only if he is excellent in math and science can I describe this student as being gifted. If he is good in English or P.E., he is not gifted; he might show talent or interest. But a really gifted student only excels in subjects that need outstanding logic.

Maria, a homeroom teacher, stated that giftedness is more prevalent "in scientific subjects… math, science … more than P.E." Christina, a mathematics teacher, illustrated this further, when asked if she would consider a student gifted if he or she were good at PE and language arts:

> P.E. no…P.E. is a talent. Language arts is a subject, so if he is good in a subject, even in English, then I guess he would be considered smart. But if he was better in the sciences, he is more gifted.

Karim, a science teacher, concurred with the opinion that perceives the gifted child as the one who excels in sciences, not language arts or PE. He explained, "No, for language arts, he should be gifted in the sciences. Also, no for P.E., because P.E. is something physical not mental…." Giftedness in these responses was considered to be more of a "mental intelligence" than a "physical intelligence." Therefore, they considered mathematics and science subjects to be ones that require more logic and intelligence than subjects like PE, which need physical stamina or even language arts. The survey responses concurred with the above findings.

In Table 5.1, 57 percent ($n = 79$) of the responses (almost half of the 140 participants) said that it was very likely that a gifted student would possess more advanced mathematics skills. Thirty-seven percent said that it was somewhat likely. Only 6 percent of the teachers responded that it was "not likely" that a gifted student would have advanced mathematical skills. This corresponds with the views that the teachers expressed in the interviews and FDGs. We can therefore conclude that a student, according to the teachers in this study, must be gifted in mathematics and the sciences in order to be considered gifted (Fig. 5.1).

Two teachers talked about what we can call the "medical doctor or engineer" syndrome, according to which gifted students are those who choose to major in engineering or medicine. Raghida, an English teacher, and Fatima, a mathematics teacher, both discussed this at great length. Raghida stated, "Lebanese people think that if you are a doctor or engineer, then it is likely you are a rocket scientist," to which Fatima added, "I do not really agree with this definition, but I think many Lebanese still think this way." The teachers' perceptions were clearly impacted by this socially constructed syndrome.

Table 5.1 Teachers' perceptions of the importance of mathematical skills

Item	Very likely No. of responses	%	Somewhat likely No. of responses	%	Not likely No. of responses	%
Possesses more advanced math skills than most students	79	57	52	37	9	6

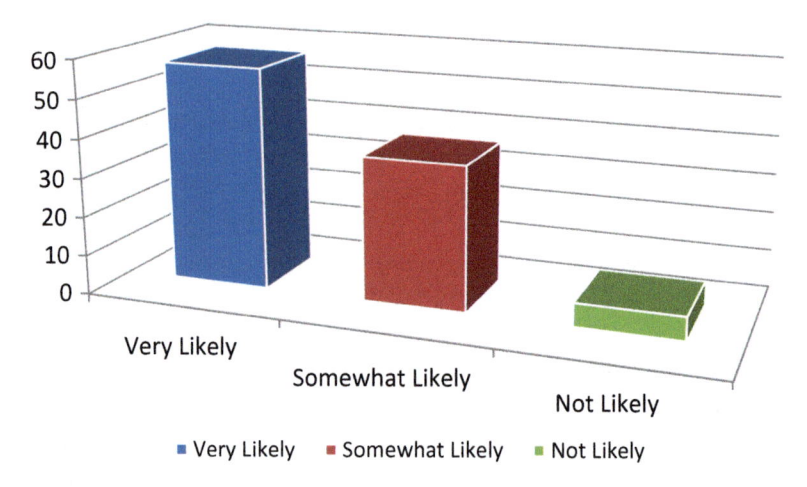

Fig. 5.1 Bar graph illustrates teachers' perceptions of gifted students' mathematical skills

5.2.4 Multiple Areas of Giftedness

According to this definition, contrary to the one above, a student can be excellent in any subject, not just in the sciences; this was prevalent across all the schools in this study. For example, language arts, music, and PE are all subjects that a student can excel in and still be considered gifted. This is because in the cases of music and language arts, for example, the student must be sufficiently creative to solve problems and come up with new ideas. For example, a teacher in one FGD in one of the schools stated:

> No, it doesn't matter, sometimes we have in learning support a student who is gifted in a special area. They are gifted. Yes, they are considered gifted if they are good in P.E. The gifted child is gifted in any subject. Doesn't matter which subject.... even P.E., in the arts. They don't have to be gifted in only [academic] studies, that's what I think.

Similarly, another FGD also focused on the view that giftedness does not necessarily mean that a student will only be gifted in the sciences. Language arts is also a subject, and if a student excels in it, then they too could be considered gifted. An English teacher explained:

5.2 Definitions of Giftedness

A long time ago, it was shameful if a student was good in language arts or grammar, but not math and science. Now, they discovered that people who excel in languages are geniuses. That is because they need creativity and logic in language arts. How much he can read and understand the concepts. Give them problem solving, and they create many ways to solve the problem.

This teacher, like three other language teachers in this study, believed that creativity is very important; hence excelling in language arts, music, art, or PE is a sure sign of giftedness.

5.2.5 Social Intelligence

To be "socially gifted" was repeatedly mentioned due to its importance in Lebanese culture. When teachers were asked what kind of giftedness would characterize the Lebanese context, the majority of them mentioned "social intelligence." The teachers in the three FGDs defined intelligence in two ways: the first, according to Lina, a science teacher, is when a child knows all about politics, religion, and history. Lina explained:

I think that the priority in Lebanon is to be gifted socially, because we have a huge lack… socially, I mean in classrooms, religion, and with accepting others etc…. This particular part is very important.

Surprisingly, the second explanation of social intelligence referred to the gifted student's ability to outmaneuver others in everyday human interactions such as cutting in line in supermarkets and negotiating the results they want. As homeroom teacher Rania explained, "socially gifted students" know a lot about "how to get ahead in the line" and "how to bargain and get a cheaper price."

Table 5.2 represents the extent to which the total number of respondents found it easy or difficult to imagine a gifted student with high social intelligence (Fig. 5.2).

As shown in Table 5.2, 87 percent of the total 140 participants from the survey responded that it was easy/very easy to imagine that a gifted student has high social intelligence. This concurred with the results in the interviews and FGDs, where the majority of the interviewees mentioned social intelligence throughout the discussions. However, when asked for recommendations for a definition of giftedness within the Lebanese context, Christina, a mathematics teacher, suggested that the Lebanese should "focus on other aspects of giftedness, other than social intelligence." Social giftedness was not considered to be the sole indicator of giftedness; however, it was considered to play a huge role in determining whether a student was gifted or not.

In the case of Lebanon, the society encourages a child to be "better than others" or "the best in class." This also means that society encourages certain behaviors, such as *shatara*شطارة in Arabic, or "outsmarting," which means having the skill to manipulate a person or a thing to obtain the desired results, usually by putting little effort into the endeavor.

Table 5.2 Teachers' perceptions of social intelligence

Item	Very easy to imagine No. of responses	%	Easy to imagine No. of responses	%	Difficult to imagine No. of responses	%	Cannot imagine No. of responses	%
Has high social intelligence (i.e., knows the names and roles of individuals in the surrounding community)	53	38	69	49	15	11	3	2

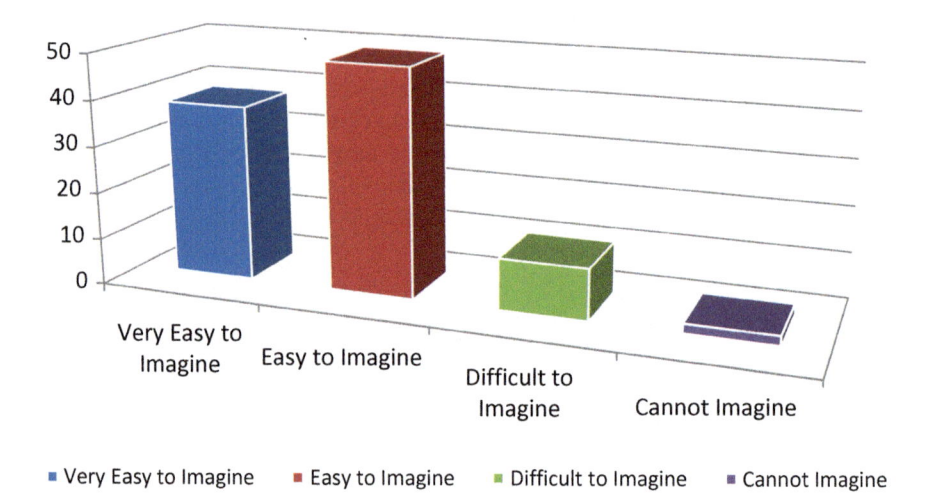

Fig. 5.2 Bar graph illustrates teachers' perceptions of gifted students having high social intelligence

5.2.6 Leadership

As already stated, although leadership was not mentioned as a defining characteristic of giftedness per se, it was mentioned throughout all the interviews and FGDs as one of the most important characteristics that a gifted student must have. Table 5.3 represents the total number of teachers who believed that leadership is an important characteristic of a gifted student (Fig. 5.3).

Teachers talked about how a gifted student takes the initiative and shows leadership in-group activities. Mathematics teacher Mira said, "The [gifted] student will take charge of the group"; Ahmad, a science teacher, added, "You feel that he is a natural born leader." This is shown as well in Table 5.3, in the "demonstrates leadership skills" section, where 82 percent of the teachers found this easy or very easy to imagine and only 18 percent of the teachers found it difficult to

5.2 Definitions of Giftedness

Table 5.3 Teachers' perceptions of leadership and communication skills

Item	Very easy to imagine No. of responses	%	Easy to imagine No. of responses	%	Difficult to imagine No. of responses	%	Cannot imagine No. of responses	%
Is a follower (seldom takes the lead)	16	12	69	49	46	33	9	6
Has poor social skills	26	19	75	54	34	24	5	3
Is shy	37	27	73	52	23	16	7	5
Cannot work independently	17	12	60	43	47	34	16	11
Demonstrates leadership skills	32	23	83	59	25	18	0	0

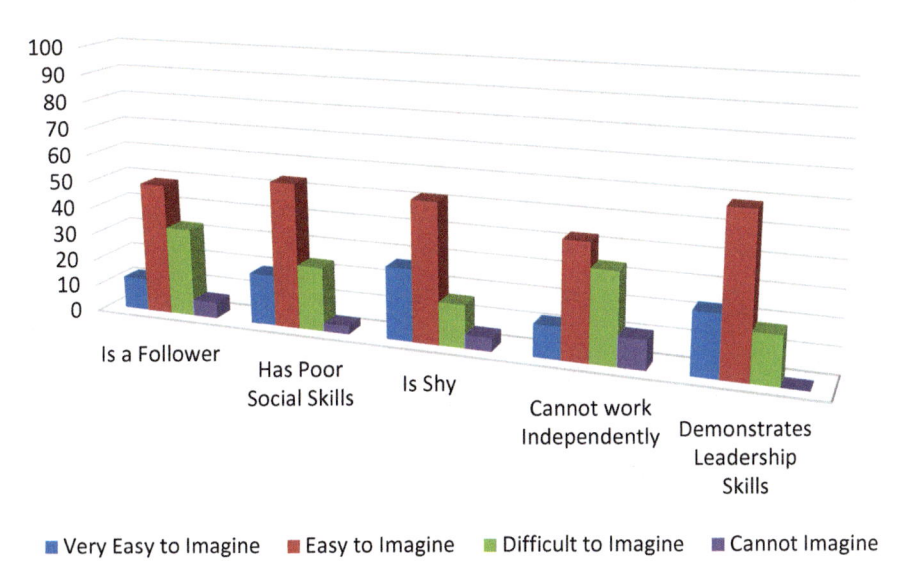

Fig. 5.3 Bar graph illustrates responses for leadership and communication skills

imagine. Not a single teacher chose "cannot imagine" with regard to a student having leadership qualities. However, with respect to the survey item "is a follower (seldom takes the lead)," 61 percent of the teachers responded that they could imagine the gifted student being a follower and not a leader, while 33 percent of the teachers had difficulty in imagining this. Only 6 percent responded as "cannot imagine." This contradicts the earlier findings that the majority of teachers believed that a gifted student has leadership qualities (Fig. 5.4).

However, in Table 5.4 almost half the participants (51 percent) responded "somewhat likely" to the characteristic of "takes the lead in small groups," and 36 percent of the teachers chose "very likely." This in turn attests to the earlier belief that gifted students show leadership qualities.

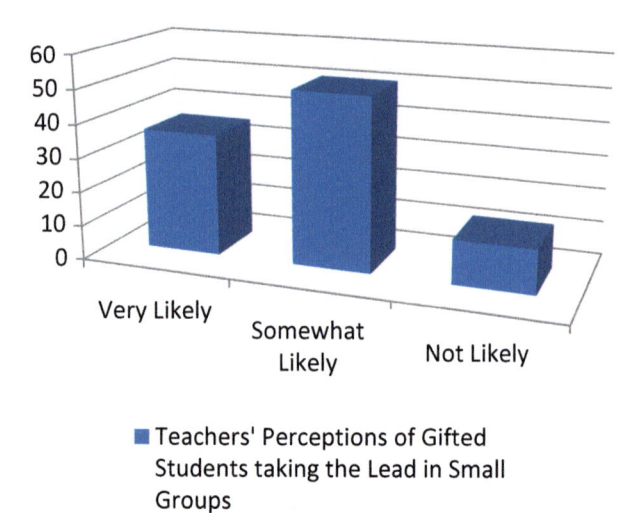

Fig. 5.4 Bar graph illustrates teachers' perceptions of gifted students taking the lead in small groups

Table 5.4 Teachers' perceptions of leadership and communication skills – continued

Item	Very likely No. of responses	%	Somewhat likely No. of responses	%	Not likely No. of responses	%
Takes the lead in small groups	50	36	72	51	18	13

5.2.7 Creativity and Problem-Solving Skills

Creativity in this study refers to asking creative questions and devising creative solutions. Like leadership qualities, creativity was mentioned throughout the interviews and FGDs and was considered a very important characteristic that a gifted student should possess (Fig. 5.5).

As Table 5.5 shows, 37 percent of the teachers found it "very easy to imagine" a gifted student who is able to create solutions to any given problem, and 57 percent of the teachers considered it "easy to imagine," which gave 94 percent of teachers. Only 6 percent of the teachers found it "difficult to imagine." To support this view, Ibrahim, a mathematics teacher, described the gifted child as:

> Someone who is so creative…. has his own way of solving problems. Very creative in solving problems, unlike other students who do it the teacher's way, and the way she taught him. Not a photocopy of the teacher.

Another mathematics teacher mentioned that the gifted child should be "genuinely creative." Many teachers considered that the creatively gifted child is the one who thinks divergently, finding more than one solution for the problem. To be creative means that one can produce "advanced answers" (Fig. 5.6).

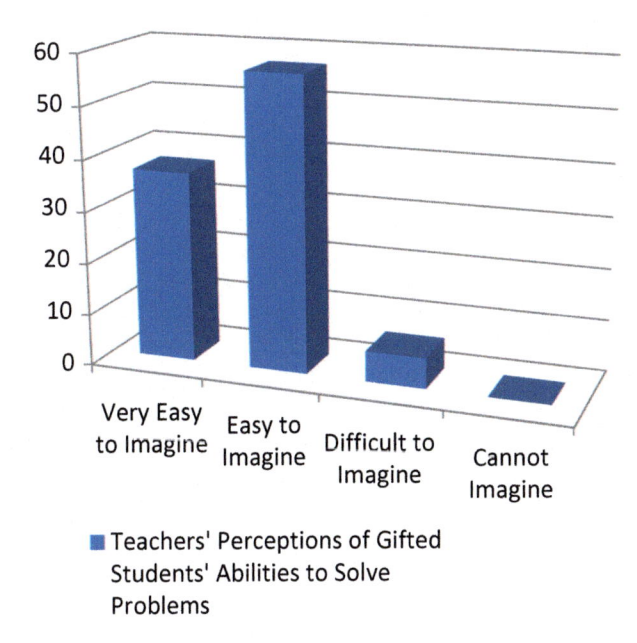

Fig. 5.5 Bar graph illustrates teachers' perceptions of gifted students' creative abilities to solve problems

Table 5.5 Teachers' perceptions of creativity and solving problems

Item	Very easy to imagine No. of responses	%	Easy to imagine No. of responses	%	Difficult to imagine No. of responses	%	Cannot imagine No. of responses	%
Can devise strategies to solve problems	51	37	80	57	9	6	0	0

Fig. 5.6 Bar graph illustrates teachers' perceptions of gifted students' ability to produce solutions

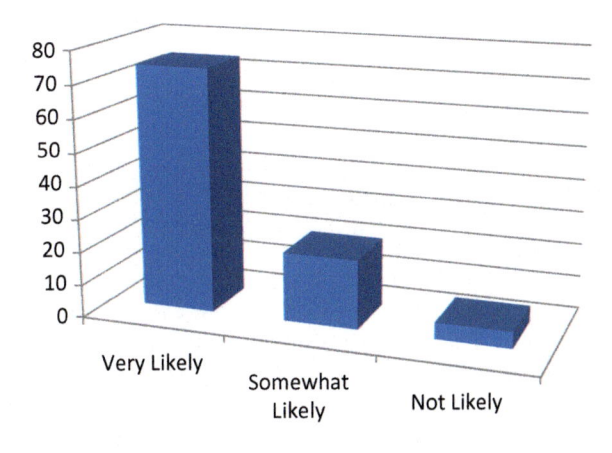

Table 5.6 Teachers' perceptions of responses to finding solutions

Item	Very likely		Somewhat likely		Not likely	
	No. of responses	%	No. of responses	%	No. of responses	%
Able to produce solutions when no one else can	103	74	30	21	7	5

To further support this view, if we take a look at Table 5.6, a total of 74 percent of the teachers considered it "very likely" that a gifted student would be able to produce solutions, while no one else could.

Lina, a science teacher, explained that a gifted child is one who "is able to create more than one solution to a problem, whether in math, or in his social life. If a student said a bad word to him, he can create a solution to this problem.... Or he can create a solution if the computer isn't working or the overhead projector." Therefore, creativity not only means being creative in the academic domain but also in real-life situations.

5.3 Characteristics and Attributes of Giftedness

This section describes all the main characteristics that surfaced during the interviews and FGDs. There were many prevalent opinions about characteristics that were shared by many elementary teachers, which helped to portray how these teachers perceived giftedness. The characteristics included being early finishers, being eager to learn/having a "thirst for knowledge," demonstrating sharpness/speediness, having a "twinkle or sparkle in the eye," having good general knowledge, being witty, and being perfectionist. There now follows a short section that discusses the physical appearance and special behaviors expected of a gifted student. Many of these items concur with the results of the survey. The tables below represent selections from sections of the survey that were mentioned in the FGDs and interviews. The figures represent the total number of responses, namely, 140, from the six schools that completed the surveys.

5.3.1 Early Finishers

One of the most frequent responses provided when participants were asked which character traits gifted students might exhibit was "they finish earlier than their classmates," or are "early finishers," or are "quick finishers." During the FGDs, all teachers mentioned this trait as an important factor in determining giftedness. If we compare this to the survey results in Table 5.7, we find that 94 percent of the teachers found it very easy to imagine/easy to imagine gifted students completing their work faster than their classmates (Fig. 5.7).

5.3 Characteristics and Attributes of Giftedness

Table 5.7 Teachers' perceptions of speediness in completing assignments

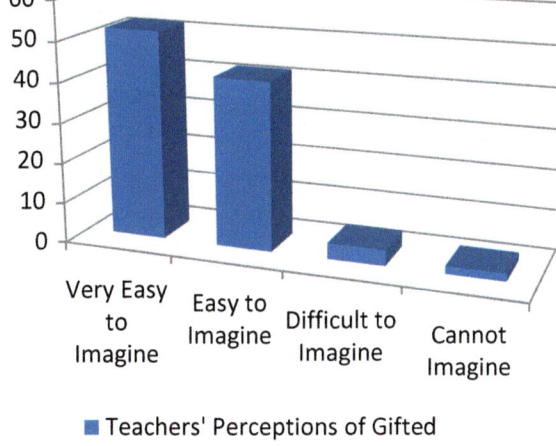

Item	Very easy to imagine No. of responses	%	Easy to imagine No. of responses	%	Difficult to imagine No. of Responses	%	Cannot imagine No. of responses	%
Completes assignments faster than same age peers	73	52	58	42	6	4	3	2

Fig. 5.7 Bar graph illustrates teachers' perceptions of gifted students' speediness in completing assignments

5.3.2 Eager to Learn or "Thirst for Knowledge"

Another common response regarding characteristics of gifted children involved being "eager to learn" and "she has a thirst for knowledge." Ahmad, a science teacher, illustrated this, saying, "You feel like they [gifted students] are so eager to learn... like they want to know everything... You can see that they have a thirst for knowledge." Seven teachers made similar comments, and this was mentioned in three FGDs. In one FGD, a teacher said, "you feel that he needs more, he needs more knowledge [and] he has a 'thirst' for knowledge and information." In order to be identified as gifted, teachers agreed that the student should have curiosity and a "thirst" for knowledge that regular students do not have.

5.3.3 Sharpness/Speediness

The word "sharp" was used in all FGDs and in three of the interviews. Most teachers described the gifted individual as "somebody who is sharp." The quickness in providing responses was regarded as another important characteristic. Many

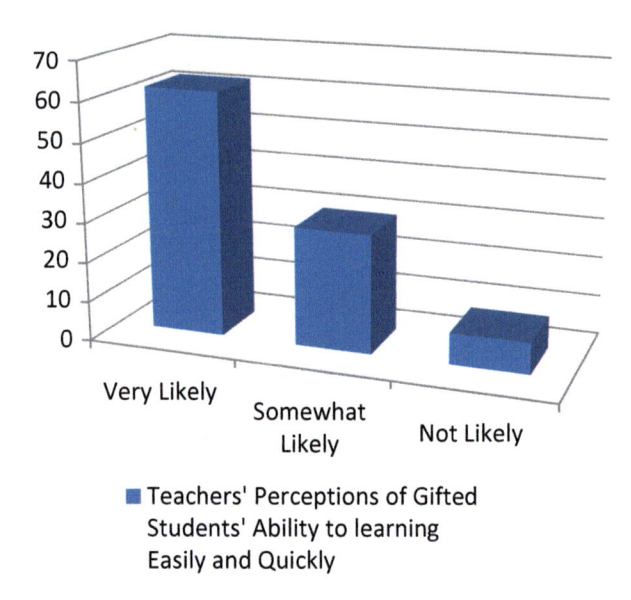

Fig. 5.8 Bar graph illustrates teachers' perceptions of gifted students' ability to learn easily and quickly

Table 5.8 Teachers' perceptions about absorbing information rapidly

	Very likely		Somewhat likely		Not likely	
Item	No. of responses	%	No. of responses	%	No. of responses	%
Learns easily and quickly	86	62	42	30	12	8

comments included "quick in answering." The teachers believed that the period between question and response should be very short.

Another frequently mentioned characteristic is the ability to "absorb information rapidly." It was another way in which teachers explained sharpness. Teachers in one FGD mentioned that a student who is gifted understands the content of the lesson immediately. Christina, a mathematics teacher, stated, "A gifted student understands what the lesson is about directly. It could be even right after I write the title on the board" (Fig. 5.8).

If we look at Table 5.8, out of the 140 respondents, 62 percent considered that a gifted student is "very likely" to learn quickly and easily, and 30 percent responded by choosing "somewhat likely." Therefore, the high majority (92%) of the teachers believed that speed in learning and completing work is one of the characteristics of a gifted student.

5.3.4 "A Twinkle or Sparkle in the Eye"

This exact phrase was mentioned many times throughout the interviews, especially in School 1. Hiba, a science teacher, said, "you can see it in their eyes… there is intelligence, like a spark! It's as if they have a twinkle in their eye." Four other teachers made similar comments. Ahmad, a science teacher, said, "You can feel it from their [eyes]… maybe a twinkle in their eyes." Karim in School 5 said, "They have a special sparkle in their eyes." Many teachers focused on the eyes and stressed that a teacher can tell whether a student is gifted or not by looking into his/her eyes.

5.3.5 General Knowledge

All teachers in the interviews and FGDs agreed that "wide general knowledge" is what characterizes gifted learners at school. Classroom participation and "knowing all the answers" are also seen as a good general knowledge indicator but in a different way. For example, Ahmad, a science teacher, said, "[The gifted learner] has to have general knowledge. For example, he will know a lot about scientific things, and even politics, religion, social things, the news, everything. He should be well informed." As Table 5.9 illustrates, 72 percent of the teachers who responded to the survey also regarded possession of wide general knowledge as an important characteristic (Fig. 5.9).

As for classroom participation, 13 of the teachers said that the students who frequently participate in class are the most able students, and their skills are apparent from the answers they give, the questions they ask, or the help they provide to other students. Teachers did not elaborate greatly on this characteristic; however, many teachers mentioned it during the FGDs.

Comments on participation were generally followed by observations about how a gifted student always knows all the answers, and this leads him/her to participate more. Mira explained, "When a student knows more than the rest, they tend to participate more than the others. Usually, gifted students know all the answers."

On the other hand, other teachers, such as Fatima and Ahmad, mathematics and science teachers, respectively, regarded this as a separate issue from that of participation, and they believed that a gifted student would always know the answer to any question. The most common response was, "He knows all the answers."

Table 5.9 Teachers' perceptions of general knowledge

Item	Very likely No. of responses	%	Somewhat likely No. of responses	%	Not likely No. of responses	%
Has a large amount of general information	101	72	32	23	7	5

```
80
70
60
50
40
30
20
10
0
      Very Likely    Somewhat    Not Likely
                      Likely

■ Teachers' Perceptions on Gifted
  Students as having a Large Amount
  of General Knowledge
```

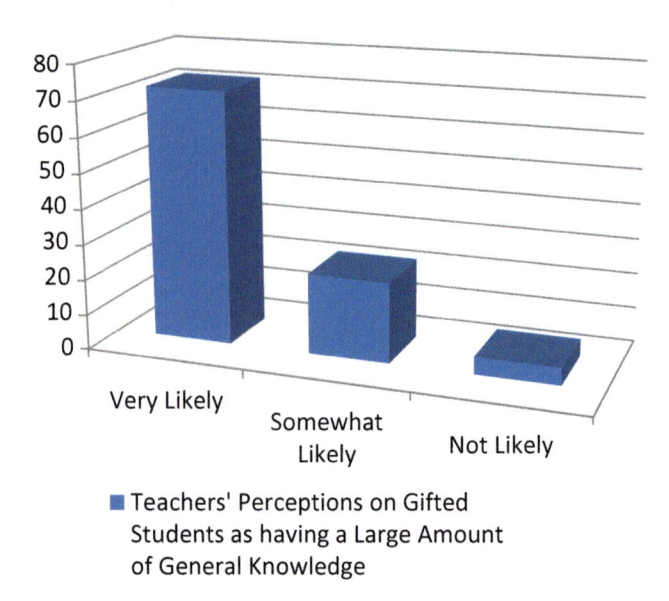

Fig. 5.9 Bar graph illustrates teachers' perceptions on gifted students as having a large amount of general knowledge

5.3.5.1 Wittiness

Teachers from two of the schools focused on the importance of "wittiness" (which refers to being funny and clever) during the interviews and FGD. Although they did not go into detail, they mentioned it casually throughout the interviews and the focus group discussions. For example, homeroom teacher Maria stated that wittiness was one of the most important characteristics and that she found wittiness to be very common among students that she perceived to be gifted.

5.3.6 Perfectionism

Three teachers mentioned perfectionism as one of the characteristics. Mira, a mathematics teacher, described the gifted child as the one who wants everything he does to be perfect. Interestingly, another teacher stated that gifted students are those who dress immaculately and are always neat and tidy and appear to be "perfect dressers." This will be discussed in further detail later.

5.3.7 Special Behavioral Characteristics

This is a very important aspect because there was much controversy regarding which behavioral traits and patterns indicated gifted individuals. Eight teachers in the interviews described the gifted student as "calm and well-mannered," while the other seven regarded gifted students as "messy and self-conceited." Other teachers from the FGDs explained that each case is different, and there is no standard behavior for a gifted. Lina, a teacher of science, explained, "He could be very calm and quiet. He could be very active. It depends." Mira made a similar observation, "It depends on the child. Behavior does not have to do with being gifted. If he's interested, he will behave. If he isn't, he will misbehave. If the lesson is repetitive, he will misbehave. I know this from last year."

A short debate that took place between two teachers during the FGDs in School 1 regarding the difference of opinion on how a gifted student behaves was as follows:

- **Teacher 1:**
  Sometimes, the giftedness can be a drawback for the student, because it puts him in a… like in a self-conceit. He becomes self-conceited. So, this is a drawback for him. He has to learn how to take himself back to reality, we have to bring him back to the fact that, okay, you are gifted, but you are not different from others.
- **Teacher 2:**
  No, on the contrary! You feel that they don't waste time, and they help the teacher. You feel as if they are your lawyer. They give a lot of energy to the class.
- **Teacher 1:**
  There are many students who are treated unfairly; they become the dynamo of the class. And they waste the class time because they always need something, and you are still explaining to the other students in the class. They are loners or they show off, and get all the teacher's attention. So they misbehave.

Three teachers perceived a gifted student as "hyper." Fatima elaborated, "My student was very hyper. He would not sit down, and when he finished first, he would get busy bullying other students. I always had to have work ready for him." Lina seconded this opinion and said that she had trouble with a "very smart student because he was extremely active and hyper, and he always disrupted the class." Other teachers emphasized the importance of the "students' style," which was explained by Susan (homeroom teacher) in terms of whether the student is "nerdy," "hyper," or "organized." Maria, a grade 2 homeroom teacher, explained that other classmates bullied her gifted student because he was perceived as a "nerd." She reported that his behavioral problems stemmed from not getting on well with other classmates because he was "smarter" than his classmates were, and so they bullied him. Bullying also occurred because he disrupted the class when he finished his class work early and consequently became bored. In Table 5.8, 78 percent of the teachers believed that gifted students misbehave in class, while only 22 percent of them found it difficult or could not imagine this. In addition, 73 percent of the teachers believed that gifted students have "poor social skills," meaning that they do not know how to "behave properly," for example, the student may interrupt the teacher while she is explaining, or he/she may bully or be bullied by another student (Fig. 5.10).

Science teacher Hiba also expressed the view that gifted students are the most polite. Table 5.10 demonstrates this as well; 57 percent of the teachers found it "somewhat likely" that gifted students are well-liked by classmates, and 47 percent of the teachers also considered it "somewhat likely" that a gifted child would behave well in class. However, only 21 percent of the teachers responded that gifted students are well-liked by classmates, and 22 percent did not consider it likely. It seems that there are differing views about how a gifted student behaves in general and there is no consensus as to how a gifted student is expected to behave in class.

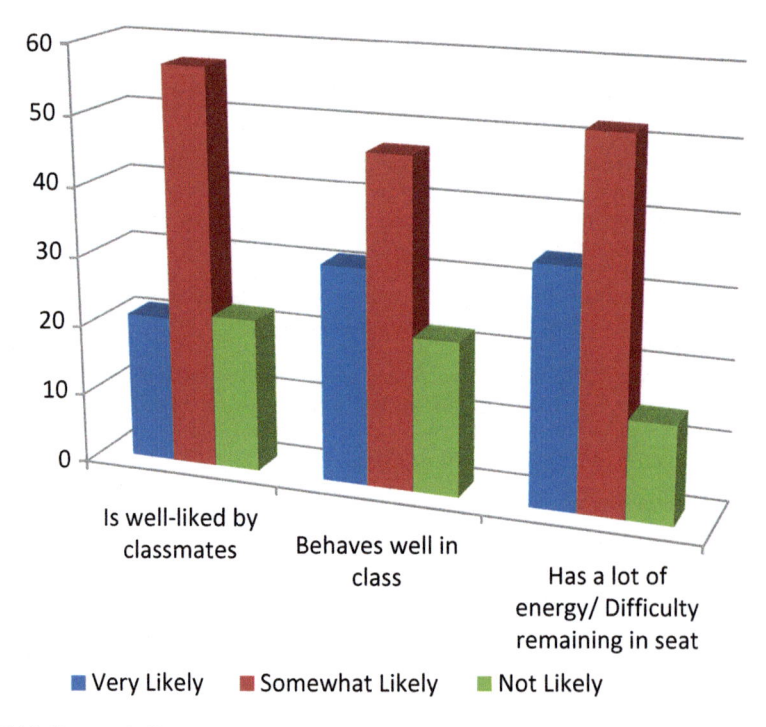

Fig. 5.10 Bar graph illustrates teachers' perceptions of behavioral characteristics

Table 5.10 Teachers' perceptions of behavioral characteristics

Item	Very likely No. of responses	%	Somewhat likely No. of responses	%	Not likely No. of responses	%
Is well-liked by classmates	29	21	80	57	31	22
Behaves well in class	44	31	65	47	31	22
Has a lot of energy and may have difficulty remaining in seat	48	34	73	52	19	14

5.3.8 Physical Appearance

Only two teachers described a gifted student as "not stylish, looks weird." Susan, a homeroom teacher, gave an example of a student in her class:

> I don't know if he's gifted; he studies a lot, and he looks weird... that's why he had many difficulties with us. First of all, jealousy. Second, he's not stylish, you know? They say that he studies a lot but he keeps not going out with us, things like that.

Ibrahim, a mathematics teacher, made a similar statement, "They [gifted children] are very unorganized. Tendency of being disorganized in their clothes... Very hectic."

Conversely, other teachers regarded gifted students as "neat and organized." Raghida described her student as "clean, healthy, organized, chooses his clothes." Karim, a science teacher, concurred with this belief and added, "He can be a very polite child or a student with a lot of manners." The rest of the teachers did not find any difference in physical appearance between a gifted student and a regular child.

5.4 Identification Procedures

This section describes the teachers' perceptions of the current identification procedures for gifted students. It includes how teachers identify their gifted students, what protocols (if any) they follow, the number of gifted students in their class (if any), and if they have ever had to refer a gifted student in their classes. These were discussed in depth during the interviews and FGDs. All the teachers responded that they had never referred a gifted student in their class for any special education considerations.

5.4.1 Current Identification Procedures

There is no official identification procedure, due to the lack of an official definition of giftedness in Lebanon. How can teachers tell if they have a gifted student in their class, and when they identify this student, what happens next? Thirteen teachers of the fifteen who were interviewed all mentioned that they would "talk to other teachers and ask their opinions." A few mentioned that they would talk to the counselor and/or principal. During the School 1 FGD, teachers mentioned that they talk with each other about their gifted students, especially during meetings and sometimes they talk to the parents concerned about their children.

Nour, a mathematics teacher, stated this problem clearly, saying, "We don't have a procedure in school. But if I were to do any procedure, I would look at the IQ, plus academics... We don't have this, but you [the interviewer] have opened our eyes to this fact."

Six other teachers also touched on this topic; however, Maria gave a more elaborate answer. She explained that gifted students are frequently not identified due to their misbehavior in class. Because they find the material easy, they start to misbehave and therefore disrupt the class. Consequently, they are not taken seriously, are frequently overlooked, and are labeled as students who misbehave. Maria added:

> Normally, the schools suffer from this, especially strict schools. They don't admit that the student is gifted, they don't admit that these kids are causing them problems. This is what happens most of the time. But they are supposed to have a special program for them, specific for gifted students to recognize them as really students who are gifted, not those who are making problems for us.

What else do the teachers look for when identifying a gifted student in their class? Fourteen of the 15 interviewees explained that they would refer to the scores on the report card. As one teacher in a FGD mentioned, "Honestly, I would see if their grades were all above 90 or 95." This statement occurred frequently throughout the discussions.

Over half of the teachers replied that they identify gifted students according to a "hunch" on their part. Two teachers, Caroline and Hiba, mentioned that they identify gifted students by those who read a lot in their classes. Caroline stated, "If he reads a lot in my class and he is a good reader, then I would identify him as gifted."

5.4.2 Gifted Girls Versus Gifted Boys

One third of the teachers' replies to the question "Are there more gifted boys or gifted girls in your class?" was that there is "no difference." The other two thirds of the teachers, all female, mentioned that there are more gifted boys than gifted girls. Lina, a science teacher, said, "I am very convinced that math and science are boys-directed. Don't get me wrong, but this is what I think." She also asserted that in general there are more gifted boys than gifted girls (Figs. 5.11 and 5.12).

Table 5.11 shows the total number of responses about subject-related giftedness with respect to boys and girls. For example, the table shows that 46 percent of respondents agreed or strongly agreed that boys are more likely to show their giftedness through activities that tap mathematical/logical abilities, whereas 48 percent disagreed or strongly disagreed with this statement. Although slightly outnumbered, almost half of the participants in the survey believed that boys have higher logical/mathematical abilities than girls do.

On the other hand, during the FGD in School 3, one teacher said, "The Lebanese consider that the male brain is bigger, but the girl uses more parts of her brain; she analyses more, much more than boys." This corresponds with the 48 percent of the respondents in Table 5.11 who disagreed that boys are more capable of logical/mathematical thinking than girls. However, it is also interesting to note that throughout all of the interviews and the FGDs, gifted students were always referred to using

5.4 Identification Procedures

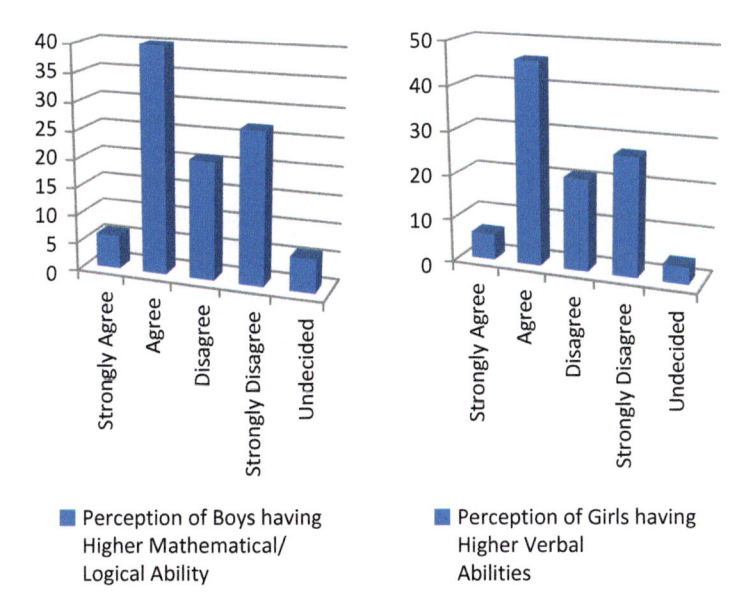

Figs. 5.11 and 5.12 Bar graphs illustrating the perception that boys have higher mathematical/logical abilities; perception that girls have higher verbal abilities

Table 5.11 Teacher's perceptions of gender differentiation (all figures are in %)

Items	Strongly agree	Agree	Disagree	Strongly disagree	Undecided
Boys are more likely to show their giftedness through activities that tap mathematical/logical ability	6	40	21	27	6
Girls are more likely to show their giftedness through activities that tap verbal abilities	6	46	17	27	4

"he" or "his." All references to giftedness applied to male students. One explanation is that they might have been using "he" as a universal pronoun.

Not surprisingly, during one FGD that took place in School 1, the teachers talked about how "only males are recognized if they are gifted in class." One math teacher during the discussion talked about how if there were a boy and a girl in her class and they were both very good at mathematics, she would identify the boy as gifted rather than the girl. If the girl was just as good, she would give credit to her parents or would be convinced that someone was helping her at home. A homeroom teacher in the same discussion added, "Gender is not a factor, is it a socially constructed male society. And these men, especially those who are gifted, become self-conceited. They should use their giftedness for 'good.'" Susan in School 2 also mentioned that Lebanese society and Lebanese school practices view gifted students as "mostly boys."

5.5 Conclusion

This study explores the existing perceptions of elementary teachers with regard to defining and identifying gifted students. This is to gain an understanding of how Lebanese teachers currently view giftedness in order to synthesize one consolidated definition as it presently exists and is generally acted upon. This was the first aim of our study – to explore the perceptions that teachers in Lebanon currently have concerning the attributes of gifted students.

We also compared documented notions of what constitutes intelligence within Western culture and African culture, versus Lebanese concepts of giftedness (specifically as reflected in current teachers' perspectives). As Serpell (2000) notes, "Giftedness includes not only a particular set of mental functions but also the value-laden concepts of appropriateness, competence, and potential" (p. 549). That is to say, each culture has its own set of values, and what might be an attribute of giftedness in one country is not necessarily the same attribute that is relevant and important in another country.

In Lebanon, social intelligence was an important characteristic consistently mentioned by the teachers. In the United States and other English-speaking industrialized societies, a person who is considered to be gifted is clever, polite, observant, critical, experimental, quick-witted, cunning, wise, judicious, and thorough (Gross, 2003). By contrast, some African tribes believe intelligence involves the possession of other cultural values, showing respect for elders, caring for young children, and showing attentiveness, understanding, trustworthiness, and obedience. Africans place more emphasis on cooperation and responsibility.

Although most teachers reported that they used report card results as a means of identification, it is important to note that there is no official identification procedure in Lebanese schools. Largely because of the absence of any official or commonly accepted *definition of giftedness*, there is no authorized, *standard identification procedure* in Lebanese schools. What usually happens, as reported by the teachers, is random and informal consultation with their colleagues or the school counselor. Most of the teachers simply identify their gifted students by means of grades and report cards.

References

Gross, M. U. M. (2003). International perspectives. In N. Colangelo & G. A. Davis (Eds.), *Handbook of gifted education* (3rd ed., pp. 547–557). Boston, MA: Allyn & Bacon.

Serpell, R. (2000). Intelligence and culture. In R. J. Sternberg (Ed.), *Handbook of intelligence* (pp. 549–577). New York, NY: Cambridge University Press.

Chapter 6
Giftedness in Lebanon: Emerging Issues and Future Considerations

Anies Al-Hroub and Sara El Khoury

Abstract This study explores the perceptions of elementary teachers in defining and identifying gifted students in order to understand how Lebanese teachers currently view giftedness and to devise a single consolidated definition. The purpose of this chapter is fourfold: to discuss the results obtained, to draw conclusions grounded in the participants' perspectives and connect them to the literature, to suggest a proposal for a policy that could be adopted with what we were able to learn from this study, and to provide implications for future research and practice.

6.1 Discussion

The first aim of our study was to explore the perceptions teachers currently have regarding the attributes of gifted students. Consequently, this section discusses the results that were obtained in relation to the two research questions from the study. It presents a discussion of the teachers' combined perceptions of gifted students and their attributes and the procedures currently used by them to identify gifted students in Lebanon at this time. Following this are the conclusions, recommendations from the teachers, proposed policy recommendations, implications, and finally the limitations of the study.

Anies Al-Hroub (✉)
Department of Education, Chairperson, American University of Beirut, Beirut, Lebanon
e-mail: aa111@aub.edu.lb

Sara El Khoury
Department of Education, American University of Beirut, Jounieh, Lebanon
e-mail: sie07@aub.edu.lb

© The Author(s), under exclusive licence to Springer International Publishing
AG, part of Springer Nature 2018
S. El Khoury, A. Al-Hroub, *Gifted Education in Lebanese Schools*,
SpringerBriefs in Psychology, https://doi.org/10.1007/978-3-319-78592-9_6

6.2 The Prevailing Lebanese Definition of Giftedness

The main themes that surfaced during the teacher interviews, focus group discussions, and surveys regarding the characteristics of giftedness were high intellectual ability, high academic performance, and social giftedness. However, no official definition of giftedness exists in Lebanon. Although the study findings gathered existing perceptions of teachers about giftedness, there was no commonly agreed definition, and many conflicting debates occurred during the FGDs.

6.2.1 High Intellectual Ability

High intelligence quotient (IQ) was a characteristic that was consistently mentioned in this study. Note that IQ is a measurement of intellectual ability, which employs a particular formula. Teachers were talking about high intellectual ability as measured by such IQ tests, and this is what they mean by "intellectual ability." Although IQ is an important factor, it is not the sole indicator of giftedness. However, many teachers believed that it was. These findings are similar to the results found by the Alencar, Fleith, and Arancibia (2009), which reveals that teachers in Argentina nominated students for gifted programs based solely on high intellectual ability and academic achievement above mean scores. These teachers perceived that academic achievement and high scores are what truly define a gifted student. This goes back to earlier definitions of giftedness, and, unfortunately, many people still rely on this definition. Hollingworth (1942), for example, believed that only the top 1% (with an IQ of 130 to 180) should be considered gifted. Moreover, regrettably, many researchers, psychologists, educators, and people in general have continued to believe right up to the present that IQ tests are a major means of determining and measuring intelligence and giftedness (Sarouphim, 1999).

Compared to the average child, the gifted student's thinking processes are both quicker and more logical (Rimm, Siegle, & Davis, 2018). Although only one teacher mentioned in this study referred to giftedness as an ability to think logically, it was included or emphasized by many teachers when they used the term "academic intelligence" or IQ.

6.2.2 High Academic Performance

Not only is this an important attribute according to the Lebanese teachers in this study, but the requirement of demonstrated high academic performance is also prevalent in the literature. For example, Silverman (1993a, 1993b, 2002, 2003) refers to intellectual giftedness as "asynchronous" development characterized by advanced cognitive abilities.

High academic performance is mentioned in most of the theories on giftedness. One of the main types of intelligence in Sternberg's (1985, 2004) triarchic theory, for example, is "analytical giftedness." Analytical giftedness is an academic talent typically measured by intelligence tests, particularly with reference to analytical reasoning and reading comprehension. Gardner's (1983) theory of multiple intelligences (MI) includes linguistic (verbal) intelligence, which involves verbal comprehension, syntax, semantics, written and oral expression, and logical-mathematical intelligence – comprising inductive and deductive reasoning, as part of his seven intelligences. These intelligences correlate with school subjects. In further definitions, according to Renzulli (1986) gifted children are "characterized by three interlocking clusters of ability, these clusters being above average (though not necessarily superior) ability, task commitment and creativity" (p. 9). Renzulli goes on to describe that above-average ability (high ability) is defined as having high levels of verbal and numerical reasoning, high levels of abstract thinking, spatial relationships, memory, and fluency. High ability is again included in the definition. Creativity can also be linked to possessing high ability. Finally, some teachers regarded high-status positions, such as that of "doctor," or logical-mathematical majors, such as engineering, to be indicators of giftedness. However, both can be linked to high IQ and high academic performance, and they can be interrelated.

6.2.3 Social Giftedness

Social giftedness was raised as an important indicator of giftedness in Lebanon. According to the current study, many teachers identified students who were "good at bargaining" and "knew all about Lebanese politics, religion, and history" as showing signs of giftedness. Perhaps this is particularly relevant because Lebanese people tend to view *shatara* ("outsmarting others") as a "very intelligent move." Therefore, as Ahmad in this study stated, if a student was able to cut in line, instead of waiting, then this would be considered doing something "extremely smart." When we look at similar studies of teachers' perceptions of giftedness conducted in Africa, for example, we find that African teachers from certain tribes place more emphasis on cooperation and responsibility. These traits were not mentioned at all by the Lebanese teachers, illustrating the fact that both cultures envision different concepts of social intelligence. Each culture has its own set of values and prioritizes different aspects of life skills that an individual needs to demonstrate in order to be considered gifted.

6.3 Characteristics and Attributes that Represent Additional Concepts of Giftedness

Creativity and leadership abilities are two other concepts of giftedness that were mentioned by the Lebanese teachers as defining characteristics. They were often interrelated by the teachers who cited creativity and leadership as characteristics of gifted children, and thus we can infer what this reveals about their concepts of giftedness. Some theorists mention creativity and leadership when discussing giftedness, for example, in 1972 a committee formed by the US Office of Education proposed a definition of giftedness that included performance domains as well as academic domains. Children could be considered gifted if they showed high abilities in creative thinking and leadership ability. Another definition refers to "creative performance, unusual leadership capacity, demonstrating high understanding in certain academic fields as well as scores on standardized tests" (Ford, Grantham, & Whiting, 2008, p. 298). Many of these attributes were also present in the Lebanese teachers' perceptions of the definition of giftedness; for example, general intellectual ability, specific academic aptitude, creative thinking, and leadership ability were often cited. Leadership and creativity are discussed in detail below, together with the other main characteristics that surfaced during the interviews and FGDs.

6.3.1 Creativity

In this study, creativity was mentioned extensively, and 131 teachers out of 140 stated that they could easily imagine a gifted student having high creative abilities. Creativity was not restricted to that displayed solely in the academic domains but also in real-life situations. The majority of the teachers who participated in this study attested to this. Therefore, creativity was found to be a prominent factor in determining giftedness, both in this study and in the literature. For example, in Renzulli's (1977) three-ring model, giftedness is an interaction between three clusters of basic traits: above-average general ability, high levels of creativity, and high levels of motivation (task commitment). In addition, in 1993, Maker proposed that creativity and intelligence could be interlinked. She stated that "creative problem-solving" is a characteristic of giftedness. She went further in 1996 to state that the key element in identifying gifted students is the ability to solve complex problems in the "most efficient, effective, or economical ways" (p. 44). This idea is likewise repeated in this study.

6.3.2 Leadership Giftedness

Teachers in one of the FGDs emphasized leadership as one of the main characteristics. The teachers talked about how the gifted student takes initiative and shows leadership in-group activities. In the other FGDs, when one teacher mentioned leadership qualities, the other teachers readily agreed and stressed its importance. Leadership is considered as important in Lebanon as it is in the literature.

Gardner (1983) suggests that a leader performs those tasks essential for the achievement of a group's goals. According to Rogers (2009), in 1972 Marland recognized two aspects of leadership in relation to giftedness: (1) the potential to lead and (2) extraordinary performance in a leadership role. The Chinese, for example, have accepted a multiple-talent concept of giftedness, valuing literacy ability, leadership, imagination, and originality (Tsuin-chen, 1961). In 1972, a committee formed by the US Office of Education proposed that children could be considered gifted if they showed high abilities in several areas, including leadership.

6.3.3 Wittiness, Sharpness (Speediness), and High Level of Critical Thinking

These characteristics were mentioned many times during the FGDs and the interviews, but they were not discussed in detail. Teachers in one of our FGDs mentioned that a student who is gifted understands the content of the lesson straight away. Renzulli (1986) mentions "automatization" of information processing, which refers to rapid, accurate, and selective retrieval of information. In other words, gifted students absorb information rapidly. This can be linked to the fact that they have more general knowledge than their peers do. All teachers in the interviews and FGDs agreed that "wide general knowledge" is what characterizes gifted learners at schools. Students who engage in classroom participation and "know all the answers" are also considered to possess broad general knowledge but are viewed differently. Such characteristics are interrelated, as shown in the responses from the teachers and FGDs that mentioned that gifted students always know all the answers, which leads them to participate more, which could be why they absorb information rapidly. A gifted student also was said to be witty, and this was considered one of the signal characteristics that differentiate a gifted student from a regular one, according to the teachers. In Aristotle's *Posterior Analytics Book 1*, for example, he claims that an intelligent person is someone who has a "quick wit." Aristotle suggested that "an intelligent person seeing someone in conversation with a man of wealth might conclude quickly that the person is seeking to borrow money from the man of wealth" (p. 9).

6.4 Identification Procedures

The identification of giftedness is very complex, loaded with controversies and debated extensively (Sarouphim & Maker, 2010). However, "identification procedures in most school districts (about 90%) in the U.S still rely heavily on the scores of standardized tests" (Ford & Harmon, 2001, p. 62). This proved to be true in this study as well. Most teachers reported that they relied on report card scores, grade levels, and IQ results.

6.4.1 Methods of Identification

No official identification procedure exists in Lebanon. The main method of identification is by means of referring to students' scores on the yearly report cards and their IQ scores. Other teachers reported that they turn to their colleagues, the school counselor, or the principal for advice when they believe that there is a gifted student in their class. On a few occasions, they discussed the possibly gifted student with the parents as well. Half of the teachers also mentioned that they rely on a "hunch" when identifying a gifted student. Only a few teachers talked about how they would identify the gifted student according to how well and how frequently they read. As Sarouphim (2010) states, Lebanon lacks the appropriate procedures to assess and identify gifted students. Moreover, Diab (2006) reports that the only tests used to assess intelligence in Lebanon are imported from the West (mostly France and the United States) and are then translated into Arabic, the native language of the Lebanese. Diab also mentions that these tests are often administered in English or French, because many Lebanese students are fluent in at least one of these two languages.

As earlier researchers such as Terman and Hollingworth based notions of giftedness entirely on raw intellectual power or IQ level (Bracken & Brown, 2006), Clinical Assessment of Behavior (CAB) (Bracken & Keith, 2004) has subsequently been added. In Germany, students are identified using the ENTER model (Ziegler & Stroger, 2004), which has five stages: explore, narrow, test, evaluate, and review. Another assessment tool that is commonly used is the *Scales for Rating the Behavioral Characteristics of Superior Students* (SRBCSS) (Renzulli, Smith, White, Callahan, & Hartman, 1976, as cited in Jarosewich, Pfeiffer, & Morris, 2002). What has sprung from this is the Gifted Rating Scales (GRS) (Pfeiffer & Jarosewich, 2003), and this more contemporary instrument has added even more scales and a comprehensive list of behavioral indicators that coincide with recent definitions of giftedness. None of these above scales are used in Lebanon.

6.4.2 Gender Identification

One of the major secondary findings is how gender plays a role in identifying giftedness in Lebanon. Two-thirds of the teachers in the study mentioned that there are more gifted boys than gifted girls. Moreover, Lebanese society and Lebanese school practices perceive boys to be far more likely to be gifted than girls. According to Freeman (2003), this is not only a Lebanese problem but also an international one: "Two boys are chosen for every girl, a strangely stable gender proportion found all over the world, from Britain to China" (p. 2). In Lee's study (2006), results also indicate "teachers tended to nominate more boys than girls." This is problematic, as Heller (2005) states, because students who are gifted may feel the continual lack of challenge in their classes. Therefore, they exhibit major behavioral problems and experience isolation due to the lack of opportunity to meet other gifted students, especially gifted girls in mathematics and sciences, but shy away from demonstrating this because of society's expectation of their gender.

6.4.3 Identification According to Behavior

It is indeed very interesting to see how different the perceptions regarding gifted students' behavior can be. In the current study, a debate took place about whether a gifted student is generally well behaved and neat or more likely to misbehave and messy. No consensus was reached as to how a gifted student will typically behave.

Many studies concur with the argument that gifted students misbehave. As supported by half of the Lebanese teachers in this study, a gifted child is one who misbehaves, disrupts the class, and interrupts the teacher. Similarly, Tobin, Wu, and Davidson (1989) provide an example of this when they discuss how teachers in the United States identify a gifted child as one who behaves antisocially at school. However, a sample of teachers and parents in Japan (another highly industrialized society) counterargued that if a gifted child is so intelligent, then he/she is expected to behave better. In concurrence with the Lebanese teachers who believed that gifted students were likely to misbehave, Gross (2003) shows that students with a very high IQ have poor social skills and such students are aware that they are greatly disliked by the other students.

On the other hand, the other half of the Lebanese teachers in this study described a gifted student as well behaved and neat. If we compare this with Terman's study, in which teachers had to identify gifted students in their class, it was found that the teachers were more likely to choose students who were better behaved. According to Hollingworth (1942), she found that students with IQs ranging from 140 to 160 tended to have more friends, were well-adjusted, and were more successful in general. This concurs with some Lebanese teachers' perceptions in this study that a gifted student is one who is "well behaved."

6.4.4 Identification According to Physical Appearance

In this study, we did not attempt to investigate specifically the perceptions of teachers regarding gifted students who come from different socioeconomic, political, or religious backgrounds. However, from what emerged in our results, teachers identified giftedness in different ways when it came to physical appearance. Some teachers discussed perfectionism in terms of the student's appearance. For example, one teacher stated that gifted students are those who dress immaculately, are always neat and tidy, and appear to be "perfect dressers"; this was how she described "perfectionism." It also explains the importance of physical appearance in the Lebanese culture. Thus, some teachers view gifted students by their "immaculate" dress. One teacher described her gifted student as clean, healthy, and organized. This relates to a study by Rimm and his colleagues (2018) which concluded that teachers were more likely to identify the "more pleasant," "well-behaved," and attractive students as gifted.

On the other hand, some teachers would identify gifted students as the ones who dress "messily" and are disorganized. Two teachers described gifted students as being "not stylish, looking weird" and having the "tendency of wearing mismatching clothes." Differences in opinions emerged greatly at what a gifted student is expected to "look like."

6.5 Conclusion

This section has focused on the two main purposes of this study: the perceived definitions of giftedness (in the absence of any official definition) and how it varies from one school to another. However, the composite definition that we present in the next paragraph is based on an amalgamation of the findings and evidence of this study, and we suggest that it represents more or less the perceptual definition that has been functioning throughout Lebanon. We also propose a working policy that could be adopted in Lebanon given their current perceptions and working gifted definition.

6.5.1 The Current Operating Definition of Giftedness in Lebanese Schools

As stated before, no official definition exists in Lebanon. Our findings portray the various perceptions that teachers currently have about giftedness. No common definition was particularly agreed upon, and many debates occurred during the FGDs. Nonetheless, we have been able to construct a current de facto definition out of these Lebanese teachers' perceptions as follows:

> Giftedness is a combination of three elements: high intellectual ability, high academic performance, and social intelligence. High intellectual ability includes exceptional ability to think logically, thus the gifted student's scores on the report cards should be the highest in the class. High academic performance means that gifted students excel in one or more subject areas. Giftedness also encompasses social intelligence, which means that the student should be a natural leader, be capable of taking charge of small groups, and be able to deal creatively and shrewdly with real-life situations, particularly those that are specifically valued in Lebanese culture.

In addition to these characteristics, a gifted student may encompass other factors such as high levels of motivation, persistence, and the ability to excel in one or more academic or nonacademic areas. In the case of Lebanon, society encourages the child to be "better than others" or to be "the best in the class." Lebanese society also advocates certain behaviors, such as *shatara* in Arabic, or "outsmarting," which means having the skill to manipulate a person or a thing (such as bargaining for a better price or cutting in line) to obtain the desired results usually while putting little effort into the endeavor. This is a combination indicator of social intelligence and creativity.

6.5.2 Lebanese Teachers' Perceptions and the Literature

This consolidated Lebanese teachers' definition above has much in common with some aspects of Renzulli's three-ring model and Sternberg's WISC model. For example, Renzulli hypothesizes that giftedness is an interaction between three clusters of basic traits: above-average general ability, high levels of creativity, and high levels of motivation (task commitment). Above-average ability and high levels of creativity were stressed in the Lebanese teachers' perceptions, for they expected a gifted student to be able to devise solutions to any problem and to possess above-average ability, which relates to high intellectual ability and high academic achievement. However, unlike Renzulli, the Lebanese teachers did not mention high levels of motivation. Renzulli discusses the importance of high task commitment as part of the interaction between the three traits, but the teachers focused more on the students' high intellectual abilities and creativity, rather than also on being highly motivated. Thus, although the Lebanese teachers' perceptions of giftedness shared some of the elements of Renzulli's model, they did not match completely. Sternberg's triarchic theory of intelligence divides intelligence into three components, namely, analytical (academic) intelligence, practical (social) intelligence, and creative (synthesis) intelligence. Recently, he has added a fourth type of intelligence, which he names WISC which is an acronym standing for *wisdom* and *intelligence synthesized* with *creativity*. Although only one teacher talked about wisdom, the other parts of Sternberg's WISC model of giftedness – namely, intelligence, and creativity – were referred to by the teachers in their discussions of high intellectual ability and the importance of creativity in relation to giftedness.

6.5.3 Misconceptions of Characteristics of Giftedness

One of the major misconceptions that emerged in the study was what we call the "doctor and engineer" syndrome, which is a socially constructed idea influenced by Lebanese culture. Contemporary definitions produced by such theorists as Renzulli, Gardner, and Sternberg indicate that there are many types of giftedness and it is not only limited to being excellent in the sciences. Another major misconception that surfaced is that there are more gifted boys than gifted girls. Perhaps this idea stems from the fact that Lebanon is a male-dominated society (although, as mentioned, this misconception prevails worldwide). When a *man* is successful, as one teacher stated, Lebanese society praises his intellect and skills, whereas if a *woman* is successful, society attributes her success to external factors that have nothing to do with the woman's intellect. However, because we are looking at the existing de facto Lebanese definition of giftedness from a cultural perspective, we cannot really suggest that Western perspectives on giftedness (embracing equal science *and* arts abilities, as well as gender neutrality) have been rejected, because, as Al-Hroub (2014) and Sarouphim (2010) state, this phenomenon has never been examined in Lebanon before. Teachers, therefore, really have no concrete pre-conceived notions of what giftedness is about. We are at a 'clean-slate' stage in the development of the definition. Further studies on students' perceptions and those of other stakeholders need to be conducted in order to really understand the misconceptions that prevail in the existing Lebanese perspective.

6.5.4 Current Identification Procedures

Regarding identification and assessment, there is no standard identification procedure for addressing gifted students because there is an absence of an official definition or even a commonly accepted definition of giftedness. What normally happens, as reported by the teachers, is that they consult with their colleagues or the school counselor. Most of the teachers shared that they identify their gifted students by means of grades and report cards. All teachers in the interviews and FGDs said that they do not have any official identification procedure in their school and none of them had ever tried to refer any gifted students to gifted programs.

6.5.5 Recommendations Made by the Teachers in this Study

Many teachers admitted that they have never thought about the issue of giftedness until now. They enjoyed the topic and said that they were willing to set up meetings about this for the next academic year. In addition, some of the teachers talked about the need for the Ministry of Education and Higher Education (MEHE) to make a standard checklist available or some other tools that teachers can use to identify gifted students and to provide facilities for teaching and supporting gifted students. One recommendation for policy-makers and decision-makers in the MEHE is to set up workshops and seminars about gifted education, so that teachers can acquire a broader definition of what giftedness entails. This way they would have a clearer idea of how to identify a gifted student in consideration with the Lebanese culture, without relying solely on scores and on report cards or focusing only on intellectual ability. Awareness campaigns about gifted education could be initiated, along with requirements for teachers to regularly update their knowledge about giftedness by consulting the literature.

School teachers recommended that they could use multiple criteria for assessing gifted students, rather than focusing only on test and IQ scores. They stated that a training program is needed in order to learn exactly how to identify a gifted student and give them what they need. The teachers also believe that the MEHE needs to promote the current gifted services and programs that are already available. Most of the teachers in this study were not aware of any existing programs for gifted students in Lebanon and therefore had no way of building upon them, so the best thing to do is start with a clean slate.

6.6 Proposal of a Lebanese Elementary School Policy for Identification of Gifted Students

This proposal is based on the context and findings of this study, which was done in the Greater Beirut Area in Lebanon. Recognizing gifted students at an early age is very important for developing a future for these students and for a better Lebanon. We believe that Lebanon should use the gifts that it has, to be able to create a better and more advanced Lebanon. Since there is no official identification procedure, we propose our own recommendations with assistance from teacher recommendations, the findings of this study, and the literature.

6.6.1 Rationale and Aims

Developing a policy to be adopted by teachers and the MEHE might aid in shedding light on giftedness in Lebanon. A number of teachers stated that this may allow the Lebanese school system to consider the gifted situation in Lebanon more carefully. As Sarouphim stated, it is not a matter of not addressing the gifted students on purpose but a matter of ignoring the situation all together. We believe that in addressing these issues, perhaps policy-makers could integrate gifted students' needs when making new policies.

Hence, the aims of the recommended policy that can be used to identify gifted students in Lebanese schools at the elementary level are as follows:

1. Include a multiple approach to identifying gifted students, moving away from relying solely on test and IQ scores.
2. Encourage the use of teacher, peer, and parental nominations to have a complete assessment of the student, which will eliminate bias, and concurrently promote the student to enter gifted programs. This procedure will more likely uncover gifted students who have been overseen by teachers, due to her or his own interpretation of what a gifted student's image should reflect.

3. Provide a more flexible and multifaceted approach to identification, in order to identify students who have learning difficulties. Include more girls in identification and include students who do not show motivation, participate regularly in class, or generally misbehave in school.
4. Administer more creativity tests, as creativity cannot be measured from cognitive tests alone.
5. Ensure that the MEHE, teachers, psychologists, special needs teachers, diagnosticians, and principals, in order for the entire Lebanese community to have similar and shared ideas of what giftedness currently entails, recognize the recommendations in this study.
6. Develop a "shared responsibility" spirit for teachers and schools regarding the gifted population. Diagnosing and identifying gifted students should not be a burden on one individual.

6.6.2 Current Operating Definition of Gifted Students in Lebanon

It has been stated throughout this study that there is no common definition of giftedness in Lebanese schools, much less in the Ministry of Education. However, in this study, we were able to conjure a current operating definition from the teachers that participated in this study. The operating definition is found in Section *6.5.1* in this chapter. However to summarize, giftedness in Lebanon focused on three main elements: (a) high intellectual ability, (b) high academic performance, and (c) social intelligence. Social intelligence refers to the student being a natural leader, is capable of taking charge of small groups, and is able to deal creatively and shrewdly with real-life situations, particularly those that are specifically valued in Lebanese culture.

6.6.3 Proposed Identification Model

The identification model we are proposing is based on a combination of the findings of this study, teacher recommendations, and the literature. The proposed identification model is more flexible and multidimensional than the standard IQ and test scores. The model also uses individually administered tests of intelligence, academic achievement, creativity tests, and dynamic tests. Creativity tests are included, because they cannot be measured solely by cognitive tests. Creativity was included as an integral element in the operating definition of giftedness, so it needs to be thoroughly tested.

We are proposing a model that was already proposed by Renzulli (1990) and Al-Hroub (2010, 2012, 2013, 2014), which is a multifaceted identification system that aims to identify all gifted characteristics, by incorporating both objective and subjective methods of identification. In this way, students could be identified whether or not they show motivation in school. This is important, because currently, motivation is not seen as a characteristic of giftedness in the Lebanese operating definition. Thus, students can still be identified whether they show motivation in school or not. It also allows other students to be identified, such as students with learning difficulties, behavioral issues, social anxiety, and so on. The following items can be integrated into what teachers are currently doing in Lebanese schools:

- Create a "talent pool," in which teachers collect all the students' scores on all types of intelligence testing. Students who score high on verbal and nonverbal testing or both, and who score at or above the 92nd percentile, would be selected. In this way, the selection is not only limited to report cards and IQ tests.
- Promote teacher nominations, as students spend most of their day with teachers, who thus would have a better idea about each student.
- In addition to teacher nominations, promote parents, peer, and self-nominations as well to eliminate the risk of bias.
- The development of a screening committee can be present in every school, where they gather the results from all the above procedures. This committee can also assess the students themselves and have interviews with them.

6.7 Implications

This section focuses on suggesting implications for practice, planning, and further research.

6.7.1 Implications for Practice and Planning

Many teachers admitted that they had never given giftedness much thought before, so at least now they have become aware of the issue of giftedness. Since the perceptions of the teachers are clearer and a definition has been developed, we can go on to provide more workshops and seminars in order to increase more teachers' awareness of gifted students' characteristics and the necessary identification procedures. More importantly, we should cater for the needs of gifted students to the best of our ability, using cultural factors and tools that are culturally sensitive.

6.7.2 Implications for Further Research

In this study, we gathered teachers' perceptions regarding giftedness and combined them to develop one clear portrayal of how Lebanese teachers currently perceive giftedness. As there is yet no one common or official Lebanese definition of giftedness, this could be seen as the starting advantage to our lack of gifted programs in Lebanon. Sarouphim (2009) labels this advantage the "clean slate phenomenon," which means that instead of untangling an established problem, we can start afresh because no programs (or even any official definition of giftedness) already exist. Since this study has helped to crystalize current views on giftedness, future research studies could include more in-depth analysis of identification procedures. This study was very general, as it asked the participants to define and identify gifted students in their classrooms. Services and programs were said to be nonexistent. Perhaps there *are* a few programs, but teachers are not aware of them. Perhaps future studies could also survey all available programs for gifted students in Lebanon. Further research is needed to learn about giftedness from the perspectives of students and parents, as well as other school stakeholders (e.g., school counselors and principals). In addition, future studies could target other school levels, for example, middle and secondary schools.

6.8 Limitations of the Study

There were various limitations to this study. It is possible that members within the same focus group discussion might have been influenced by what their colleagues were saying or that they might have given responses to please their colleagues or sway their views. In addition, some teachers would not agree to be audiotaped in the interviews, so we had to make sure that we recorded all that was said by hand. Another almost inevitable limitation is that there were more females than males in the study, which might have influenced the results. However, because most teachers at the elementary level in Lebanese schools are females, there might not be such a skewed representation in the higher grades where male teacher numbers are significantly higher. It would be better next time to include school counselors and principals in the study, particularly at the elementary level possibly to help increase the number of male participants; however their inclusion at all grade levels would be desirable as counselors and principals are important school stakeholders.

A specific limitation to this study is that it was conducted in private schools only. Although private schools have the advantage that there is a large population of bilingual teachers who are exposed to different cultures, they are not representative of all Lebanese schools. It would benefit the study to also interview teachers from public schools, as gifted students are found everywhere, not just in private schools. In addition, this study was conducted in the Greater Beirut Area only. Because this study was about teachers' perceptions of giftedness in Lebanon, it would have been better to include more cities and towns across a wider catchment area. Finally, we only aimed to study elementary schools. Although we made clear the reason for choosing elementary teachers in our study, it would be helpful to investigate the perceptions of teachers at intermediate and secondary school levels as well.

References

Alencar, E. M. L. S., Fleith, D. S., & Arancibia, V. (2009). Gifted education and research on giftedness in South America. In L. Shavinina (Ed.), *International handbook of giftedness* (pp. 1491–1506). New York: Springer.

Al-Hroub, A. (2010). Developing assessment profiles for mathematically gifted children with learning difficulties in England. *Journal of Education for the Gifted, 34*(1), 7–44.

Al-Hroub, A. (2012). Theoretical issues surrounding the concept of gifted with learning difficulties. *International Journal for Research in Education, 31*, 30–60.

Al-Hroub, A. (2013). Multidimensional model for the identification of gifted children with learning disabilities. *Gifted and Talented International, 28*, 51–69.

Al-Hroub, A. (2014). Identification of dual-exceptional learners. *Procedia-Social and Behavioral Science Journal, 116*, 63–73.

Bracken, B. A., & Brown, E. F. (2006). Behavioral identification and assessment of gifted and talented students. *Journal of Psychoeducational Assessment, 24*(2), 112–122.

Bracken, B. A., & Keith, L. K. (2004). *CAB, Clinical Assessment of Behavior: Professional manual*. Psychological Assessment Resources: PAR.

Diab, R. (2006). University students' beliefs about learning English and French in Lebanon. *Systems, 34*(1), 80–96.

Ford, D. Y., Grantham, T. C., & Whiting, G. W. (2008). Culturally and linguistically diverse students in gifted education: Recruitment and retention issues. *Exceptional Children, 74*(3), 289–306.

Ford, D. Y., & Harmon, D. A. (2001). Equity and excellence: Providing access to gifted education for culturally diverse students. *Journal of Secondary Gifted Education, 12*(3), 141–141.

Freeman, J. (2003). Gender differences in gifted achievement in Britain and the USA. *Gifted Child Quarterly, 47*(3), 202–211.

Gardner, H. (1983). *Frames of mind: The theory of multiple intelligences*. New York: Basic Books.

Gross, M. U. M. (2003). International perspectives. In N. Colangelo & G. A. Davis (Eds.), *Handbook of gifted education* (3rd ed., pp. 547–557). Boston: Allyn & Bacon.

Heller, K. (2005). The Munich model of giftedness designed to identify and promote gifted students. In R. J. Sternberg & J. E. Davidson (Eds.), *Conceptions of giftedness* (2nd ed., pp. 147–170). New York: Cambridge University Press.

Hollingworth, L. (1942). Children above 180 IQ. *The Teachers College Record, 44*(1), 56–56.

Jarosewich, T., Pfeiffer, S. I., & Morris, J. (2002). Identifying gifted students using teacher rating scales: A review of existing instruments. *Journal of Psychoeducational Assessment, 20*(4), 322–336.

Lee, L. (2006). Teachers' conceptions of gifted and talented young children. *High Ability Studies, 10*(3), 183–196.

Pfeiffer, S. I., & Jarosewich, T. (2003). *Gifted rating scales*. San Antonio, TX: Psychological Corporation.

Renzulli, J. S. (1977). *The enrichment triad model: A guide for developing defensible programs for the gifted and talented*. New York: Creative Learning Press.

Renzulli, J. S. (1986). The three-ring conception of giftedness: A developmental model for creative productivity. In R. J. Sternberg & J. Davidson (Eds.), *Conceptions of giftedness* (pp. 53–92). New York: Cambridge University Press.

Renzulli, J. S. (1990). A practical system for identifying gifted and talented students. *Early Childhood Development, 63*(2), 9–18.

Rimm, S., Siegle, D., & Davis, G. (2018). *Education of the gifted and talented* (7th ed.). Boston, MA: Pearson.

Rogers, K. B. (2009). Leadership giftedness: Is it innate or can it be developed? In L. V. Shavinina (Ed.), *International handbook on giftedness* (pp. 633–645). New York: Springer.

Sarouphim, K. M. (1999). Discovering multiple intelligences through a performance-based assessment: Consistency with independent ratings. *Exceptional Children, 65*(2), 151–161.

Sarouphim, K. M. (2009). The use of a performance assessment for identifying gifted Lebanese students: Is DISCOVER effective? *Journal for the Education of the Gifted, 33*(2), 275 295.

Sarouphim, K. M. (2010). A model for the education of gifted learners in Lebanon. *International Journal of Special Education, 25*(1), 71–79.

Sarouphim, K. M., & Maker, C. J. (2010). Ethnic and gender differences in identifying gifted students: A multi-cultural analysis. *International Education, 39*(2), 42–48.

Silverman, L. K. (1993a). *Counseling the gifted and talented*. Denver: Love.

Silverman, L. K. (1993b). Counseling needs and programs for the gifted. In K. A. Heller, F. J. Mönks, & A. H. Passow (Eds.), *International handbook of research and development of giftedness and talent* (pp. 631–647). New York: Pergamon.

Silverman, L. K. (2002). Asynchronous development. In M. Neihart, S. M. Reis, N. M. Robinson, & S. M. Moon (Eds.), *Social and emotional development of gifted children: What do we know?* (pp. 145–153). Washington, DC: National Association for Gifted Children.

Silverman, L. K. (2003). Gifted children with learning disabilities. In N. Colangelo & G. A. Davis (Eds.), *Handbook of gifted education* (3rd ed., pp. 533–543). Boston: Allyn & Bacon.

Sternberg, R. J. (1985). *Beyond IQ: A triarchic theory of human intelligence*. Cambridge, MA: Cambridge University Press.

Sternberg, R. J. (2004). *International handbook of giftedness*. Cambridge: Cambridge University Press.

Tobin, J. J., Wu, D. Y. H., & Davidson, D. H. (1989). Preschool in three cultures: Japan. In *China and the United States*. New Haven, CT: Yale University Press.

Tsuin-chen, O. (1961). Some facts and ideas about talent and genius in Chinese history. In G. Z. F. Bereday & J. A. Lauwerys (Eds.), *Concepts of excellence in education: The yearbook of education* (pp. 213–221). New York: Harcourt, Brace & World.

Ziegler, A., & Stroger, H. (2004). Identification based on ENTER within the conceptual frame of the actiotope model of giftedness. *Psychology Science, 46*(3), 324–241.

Appendix A: Perceptions of Giftedness Survey

I. *Demographics*

Please indicate your answer by circling the corresponding number.

1. Gender

Male	01
Female	02

2. How many years have you taught in total in the nearest year? Please include part-time teaching if applicable. _____
3. What is the *highest level* of education you have completed? Please encircle only *one* number.

(a) High school certificate	01
(b) Bachelor's	02
(c) Education specialist or professional diploma based on at least 1 year of course work past a master's degree level	03
(d) Master's	04
(e) Doctorate	05
(f) Others (please specify) _____	06

4. In what areas are you certified? Please encircle *one* number on each line.

	Yes	No
(a) Childhood education	01	02
(b) Elementary education	01	02
(c) Secondary education	01	02

(continued)

(continued)

	Yes	No
(d) Special education	01	02
(e) English education	01	02
(f) Science education	01	02
(g) Math education	01	02
(h) Others (please specify) _____	01	02

5. What subject do you teach? _____

II. *Conceptions and Definitions of Giftedness*

In the following set of items, decide how easy it is for you to imagine a gifted elementary student who has the stated characteristics by circling the appropriate number. For example, if it is easy for you to imagine a gifted elementary student who learns at a slow pace, then encircle 4 which represents "Very easy to imagine." If you cannot imagine a gifted elementary student who learns at a slow pace, then encircle 1 which represents "Cannot imagine."

1. How easily can you imagine a gifted elementary student who…?

	Very easy to imagine	Easy to imagine	Difficult to imagine	Cannot imagine
1. Learns at a slow pace	4	3	2	1
2. Transfers learning into other subjects or real-life situations	4	3	2	1
3. Has difficulty with reasoning skills (such as seeing connections between ideas, solving problems without help)	4	3	2	1
4. Has high social intelligence (i.e., knows the names and roles of individuals in the surrounding community)	4	3	2	1
5. Is a follower (seldom takes the lead)	4	3	2	1
6. Has poor social skills	4	3	2	1
7. Works hard	4	3	2	1
8. Has a short attention span	4	3	2	1
9. Pays attention to detail	4	3	2	1
10. Is shy	4	3	2	1
11. Misbehaves in school	4	3	2	1
12. Has a large store of general knowledge	4	3	2	1
13. Is not motivated	4	3	2	1
14. Can successfully carry out multiple verbal instructions	4	3	2	1
15. Completes assignments faster than same age peers	4	3	2	1
16. Tries to understand the how and whys of things	4	3	2	1

(continued)

Appendix A: Perceptions of Giftedness Survey

(continued)

	Very easy to imagine	Easy to imagine	Difficult to imagine	Cannot imagine
17. Has skill deficits in one or more academic area	4	3	2	1
18. Cannot work independently	4	3	2	1
19. Has unusual interests for their age (e.g., they take interest in studying the weather and walled cities)	4	3	2	1
20. Demonstrates leadership skills	4	3	2	1
21. Dislikes drills and practice	4	3	2	1
22. Is bilingual	4	3	2	1
23. Can devise strategies to solve problems	4	3	2	1

2. In the following set of items, we would like you to focus on your personal beliefs. Indicate your level of agreement by encircling the corresponding number.

	Strongly agree	Agree	Disagree	Strongly disagree	Undecided
1. The potential for giftedness is present in equal proportions in all cultural/sectarian/political groups in our Lebanese society	5	4	3	2	1
2. The potential for giftedness is present in equal proportions in all socioeconomic groups in our Lebanese society	5	4	3	2	1
3. Boys are more likely to show their giftedness through activities that tap mathematical/logical ability	5	4	3	2	1
4. Girls are more likely to show their giftedness through activities that tap verbal abilities	5	4	3	2	1

III. *Characteristics and Prevalence*

For the following sets of items, imagine that you have been asked to identify gifted students in your classroom. Indicate how likely you would be to identify a student as gifted if that student exhibited the following characteristics, by encircling the number corresponding to your response.

1. How likely would you be to identify a student as gifted if the student…?

	Very likely	Somewhat likely	Not likely
1. Learns easily and quickly	3	2	1
2. Uses details in stories and pictures	3	2	1
3. Has an advanced vocabulary for age	3	2	1
4. Has a large amount of general information	3	2	1

(continued)

(continued)

	Very likely	Somewhat likely	Not likely
5. Has high interest in specialty topic	3	2	1
6. Possesses more advanced math skills than most students	3	2	1
7. Has a high interest in school	3	2	1
8. Uses expressive language	3	2	1
9. Is easily bored with routine tasks	3	2	1
10. Can carry out a multistep command	3	2	1
11. Asks a lot of questions	3	2	1
12. Can apply his/her understandings of concepts in new contexts	3	2	1
13. Able to produce solutions when no one else can	3	2	1
14. Has unusual emotional understanding	3	2	1
15. Is self-motivated	3	2	1
16. Is able to see another's point of view	3	2	1
17. Is well liked by classmates	3	2	1
18. Likes to work alone	3	2	1
19. Has an awareness of issues related to his/her community	3	2	1
20. Takes the lead in small groups	3	2	1
21. Is flexible in the face of change	3	2	1
22. Behaves well in class	3	2	1
23. Has a lot of energy and may have difficulty remaining in seat	3	2	1

2. Please answer the following questions:

    (a) What is the total number of students in your class(es)?
    _____

    (b) In your opinion, what is the number/ratio of gifted students in your class(es)?
    _____

    (c) In your opinion, how many of your students can be identified and labeled as gifted? _____

- We are planning to conduct focus group discussions with teachers in schools and would like to know if this participant is interested in this discussion. Please tick one of the following:

    Yes ____   No ____

- We are planning to conduct individual interviews with teachers in schools and would like to know if this participant is interested in this discussion. Please tick one of the following:

    Yes ____   No ____

Appendix B: Protocol of Focus Group Discussion with Teachers

1. *Purpose of the Focus Group Discussion* (2 minutes)
2. *Introduction of Participants and Facilitators* (5 minutes)

Good morning, and welcome to our focus group session on teachers' perceptions of giftedness. Thank you for taking the time to come here. We would like to understand your views on giftedness and what determines whether a student is gifted or not in your opinion. Remember, there are no right or wrong answers but rather your perceptions. Please feel free to share your point of view even if others share a different perception or outlook. Before we start, allow me to remind you to please talk one at a time and to keep in mind that I am interested in everything you have to say, whether it is positive or negative. All comments are helpful.

Our session will last between 90 and 120 minutes. Before we begin, we would like to get to know more about you. Hello, please tell me your name and how long you have been teaching.

3. *Discussion Themes*

Theme 1: Definition of Giftedness
Guide question(s):

- How does your school define giftedness?
- What is your recommendation for the definition of giftedness in the Lebanese context?
- What would the definition include and what are its components?
- How would you define a gifted child? If you were to come up with a definition that is relevant to the Lebanese context right now, what would it be?

Theme 2: Characteristics
Guide question(s):

- How do you identify the gifted students in your class?
- What are the characteristics that you look for when identifying a student as being gifted?

- What sort of behavior do you expect your gifted student to have?
- How does a gifted person look like?
- If a student excelled in the language arts, would you consider them as being gifted?

Theme 3: Prevalence
Guide question(s):

- How many gifted students are there in your class?
- Are there more gifted boys or gifted girls in your class?

Theme 4: Current Identification Practices
Guide question(s):

- What are the current practices in identifying the gifted students in your class? For example, is there a type of protocol that you follow?
- Does your school identify students as gifted at the kindergarten/elementary level?
- Describe a student that you consider(ed) gifted. Include his/her characteristics and what particularly stood out about him/her that led you to think s/he was gifted.
- How do you assess your students for giftedness?
- Have you ever had to refer a gifted student in your class? If yes, what was the procedure?

Theme 5: Curricular and Program Services
Guide question(s):

- What are the available curricular and program services for gifted students in your school?
- What sort of activities does your school offer students with different talents (e.g., talent shows, acceleration, grade skipping, tracking, show and tell, etc.)?
- Do you have any referral services in your school?
- Do you have resource rooms? What kind of activities do you have for enhancing highly able students?

4. *Summary of Discussion Points* (10 minutes)

Thank you for participating in this study. All the information here is confidential. Would you like to add anything further?

Appendix C: Teacher Interview Protocol

- Good morning, and welcome to our interview session on teachers' perceptions of giftedness. Thank you for taking the time to come here. We would like to understand your views on giftedness and what determines whether a student is gifted or not in your opinion.
- Remember, there are no right or wrong answers but rather your perceptions. Please feel free to share your point of view even if others share a different perception or outlook.
- Before we start, allow me to remind you that I am interested in everything you have to say, whether it is positive or negative. All comments are helpful.
- Our session will last about an hour. Before we begin, we would like to get to know more about you. Hello, please tell me your name and how long you have been teaching.

Definition and Concepts
- How would you define giftedness in general?
- Would you consider a student as being gifted if he/she excelled in language arts? What about PE?
- Do you have a common definition of giftedness in your school?
- How would you define a gifted child? If you were to come up with a definition that is relevant to the Lebanese context right now, what would it be?
- What is your recommendation for a definition of giftedness within the Lebanese context?

Characteristics and Prevalence
- What are the main characteristics a gifted student should have in your opinion?
- What are the attributes that you look for when identifying that student has gifted?
- What sort of behaviors does the gifted student exhibit?
- How does a gifted person look like?
- How many gifted students are in your class?
- Were there more gifted boys or girls in your class?

Identification and Assessment
- How do you identify the gifted students in your class?
- Is there any procedure that you follow?
- How do you assess your students for giftedness?

Services and Programs
- Do you have any curricular or program services available in your school? (If yes, please specify.)
- Do you have any referral services in your school? (If yes, please specify.)
- As a teacher, what do you do when you feel that you have a gifted student in your class?
- Have you ever had to refer a gifted student in your class? If yes, what was the procedure?
- Do you have any resource rooms? What kind of activities do you have for enhancing highly able students?

Index

A
Academic performance, 76–78, 96–97, 106
American Psychological Association, 17
American University of Beirut (AUB), 3
Ancient Greece, 23
Arab Council for the Gifted and Talented (ACGT), 3

C
Clinical Assessment of Behavior (CAB), 45, 100
Cognitive Abilities Test (CogAT), 43
Cognitive-deficit hypothesis, 19
Commissioner of Education, 10
Communication skills, teachers' perceptions, 81, 82
Conformability, 71
Creativity, 82, 83
Credibility, 70
Cultural factors, 32
Culture as a language, 18

D
Dependability, 71

E
ENTER model, 100

F
Focus group discussions (FGDs), 63, 65–67, 69, 115–116

G
Gagné's Differentiated Model of Giftedness and Talent, 15
Gardner's theory, 13, 15
General Certificate in Secondary Education (GCSE), 53
Gifted learners, 28–32
    characteristics and attributes
        academic fields, 98
        asynchronous development, 29
        children, 28
        chronological development, 30
        cognitive aptitudes, 28
        concepts of giftedness, 98
        creativity, 98
        emotional stability tests, 29
        intellectual, 29
        intrinsic mental readiness, 30
        leadership giftedness, 98–99
        Lebanese teachers' perceptions, 98
        logical thinking, 30
        Lombroso's declaration, 29
        motivation, 30, 31
        musical memory, 30
        non-intellective (affective) elements, 31
        precocious language and thought, 29
        self-concept and self-creating goals, 32
        self-regulatory, 32
        social skills, 31
        socioeconomic factor, 29
        verbal and conceptual skills, 30
        wittiness, sharpness (speediness) and level of critical thinking, 99
Gifted Rating Scales (GRS), 44, 100

Giftedness, 10, 13, 14, 21–28, 84–93
  above-average ability, 11
  academic performance, 10
  achievement, 11
  adulthood, 12
  aptitude domains, 15
  areas, 78–79
  attributes, 14
  characteristics and attributes
    in class, 90
    early finishers, 84–85
    FGDs, 89
    general knowledge, 87–88
    homeroom teacher, 89
    perfectionism, 88
    physical appearance, 91
    sharpness/speediness, 85–87
    teachers' perceptions, 90
    thirst for knowledge, 85
    twinkle/sparkle in eye, 87
    wittiness, 88
  conceptions, 11
    China, 25
    Europe, 23–24
    Middle East, 21–23
    New Zealand, 25
    South Africa, 26
    teachers, 26–28
    Turkey, 24–25
  creation, 74–75
  creative problem-solving, 11
  and culture, 13, 18–19
  definitions, 74–84
  demotivation/environmental factors, 15
  diverse procedures, 10
  elements, 13, 15
  explicit/implicit theories, 14
  FGDs, 73, 74
  gifted and talented children, 11
  groups of individuals, 12
  high academic performance, 76–78
  high intellectual ability, 75
  high-level thinking, 11
  identification (see Identification procedures)
  intellectual and creative ability, 15
  intelligences
    bodily-kinesthetic, 13
    interpersonal, 13
    intrapersonal, 13
    linguistic (verbal), 13
    logical-mathematical, 13
    musical, 13
    naturalist, 13
    spatial, 13
  IQ tests, 11
  leadership and communication skills, 80–82
  in Lebanese schools, 94
  linguistic and logical-mathematical abilities, 11
  nonintellectual traits, 12
  nurturing, 16–18
  personal/societal beliefs and experiences, 20
  problem-solving skills, 82–84
  pyramid-shaped model, 15
  social intelligence, 79, 80
  stages
    empirical, 10
    metaphysical, 10
    theological approach, 10
  survey, 111–114
  and talent, 12, 15
  task commitment, 12
  thought, 12
  three-ring model, 11
  traditional intelligence test, 15
  types
    analytical, 13
    practical, 14
    synthetic, 14
  underrepresentation, cultural factors, 19–20
  The United States, 94
  Western and African culture vs. Lebanese concepts, 94
  WICS model, 14
The Gulistan, 21, 22

I

Identification procedures
  African-American and Hispanic-American students, 55
  case of labeling, 40
  in class, 91
  current, 91–92, 104
  educational programs, 55
  gender, 100–101
  gender role expectations, 40
  gifted girls vs. boys, 92–93
  giftedness and gender, 53–54
  intelligence testing, 40–42
  in Lebanese schools, 102–103
  Lebanese teachers' perceptions and literature, 103
  methods, 100
  in Middle East, 48
  minority groups, 48–50

misconceptions and misdiagnosis, 50–51, 103–104
physical appearance, 101–102
racist predispositions, 51–52
recognition of individuals, 39
in school districts, 99
socioeconomic biases, 51–52
SRBCSS and attitude surveys, 55
stereotyping, 52, 53
students' behavior, 39, 101
teachers, 104–105
tools, 43–48
working policy, 102
Individualized Education Plan (IEP), 4
Intellectual ability, 74, 75
Intelligence quotient (IQ), 96
  scores, 2, 11, 32
  tests, 41, 43
Intelligence testing, 40–42
International Center for Excellence and Innovation (ICEI), 3
Iranian hierarchical wisdom model (IHW), 22

K
Kaufman Test of Educational Achievement, Second Edition (KTEA-II), 43

L
Leadership, 80–82
  and creativity, 98
  giftedness, 98–99
Lebanese American University (LAU), 4
Lebanese definition of giftedness
  academic performance, 96–97
  intellectual ability, 96
  social giftedness, 97
  teacher interviews, 96
Lebanese elementary school policy
  current operating definition, 106
  identification model, 106, 107
  rationale and aims, 105–106
Lebanon, 1–4
  aims, 5
  definition of giftedness, 1, 6
  elementary teachers, 5
  gifted education
    clean slate phenomenon, 2
    educational institution, 3
    grade-based acceleration, 2
    learning disabilities, 2
    legislative framework, 2
    national school curriculum, 1

private schools, 2
procedures, 2
students' intellectual ability and IQ tests, 2
Western literature, 2
giftedness, 5
growing interest, 5
identification procedures, 4, 5
implications
  elementary schools, 108
  further research, 107–108
  Lebanese schools, 108
  practice and planning, 107
  private schools, 108
practical implication, 6
qualitative research techniques, 6
solid-based theory and evidence, 6
talented and gifted education
  AUB, 3
  challenges, 3
  course requirements, 4
  learning disabilities, 4
  learning outcomes, 3
  opportunities, 3
  resources, 4
  teachers' conceptions, 5
  theoretical implication, 6

M
Mathematical skills, teachers' perceptions, 78
Mental manager, 14
Ministry of Education and Higher Education (MEHE), 2, 3, 104–106
Misconceptions of giftedness, 50–51
Misdiagnosis, 50–51
Multiple intelligences (MI), 97
Munich Model of Giftedness (MMG), 18

N
Nongovernmental organizations (NGOs), 3
Notre Dame University – Louaize (NDU), 4

O
Otis-Lennon School Abilities Test (OLSAT), 43

P
Palestinians, 22
Perceptions of Giftedness Survey, 64
Physical education (PE), 77

Q
Qualitative research method, 26

R
Rating scales, 44, 46, 48, 50, 55
Renzulli's three-ring model, 12, 103

S
Scales for Rating the Behavioral Characteristics of Superior Students (SRBCSS), 44
Scholastic Aptitude Test (SAT), 45
Self-management techniques, 23
Social contract, 23
Social giftedness, 96, 97
Social intelligence, 79, 80
Stanford-Binet Intelligence Scale, 43
Star Model, 13
Stereotyping, 52, 53
Sternberg's WISC model, 15, 103

T
Task commitment, 12
Teacher interview protocol
   definition and concepts, 117
   characteristics and prevalence, 117
   identification and assessment, 118
   services and programs, 118
Teachers' perceptions, 64–70
   aims, 62
   data analysis, 70
   data collection
      FGDs, 65–67, 69
      interviews and FDGs, 64
      perceptions of giftedness survey, 64–65
      procedure, 69–70
      semi-structured interviews, 67–69
      survey, 68
   disabilities, 62
   educational programs, 61
   educational services, 63
   elementary school level, 62
   gender and school, 63
   participants, 63–64
   private schools, 62
   research design, 62
   research questions, 62
   trustworthiness, 70–71
Terman's study, 42
Transferability, 71

W
WICS model of giftedness, 14
Wisdom, 22
World Council for Gifted and Talented Children (WCGTC), 3

Z
Zone of proximal development (ZPD), 45